A Gaza Diary

Not in a Vacuum

FELICITY HEATHCOTE

About the author

Felicity Heathcote, a Dublin-based clinical psychologist, teacher and writer has spent several years in Palestine where she conducted workshops for UNRWA and other non-governmental groups in Gaza and the West Bank. Born in England, she has also worked in Iran, Japan, Saudi Arabia, the USA and Ireland. The Official Psychologist to the Irish Olympic team for Barcelona, Sydney and Athens, she applies her adapted zen techniques to sport, business, the arts and education. Her publications include Peak Performance: Zen and the Sporting Zone (1996) and The Learning Zone (2000), both published by Wolfhound Press and The Resting Place Of The Moon (2006) and The Man With No Secrets (2010) published by OtherWorld Press. Committed to human rights and the dignity of the person, she hopes that this diary will show the truth of the suffering in Gaza.

To the people in Palestine, and to all who have suffered and who continue to suffer in this conflict

This diary is a record of some of the terrible sufferings of the people of Gaza over decades. Nothing has really changed since the winter of 2008/9 other than the scale of the death and destruction. At the time of writing, the numbers of dead and missing in 2023/4 has now risen to over thirty thousand. The injuries, especially those of the children, are unbearable to contemplate and there is still no end in sight, no sign yet of a permanent ceasefire.

A Gaza Diary

Not in a Vacuum

FELICITY HEATHCOTE

June 2024

Breaking the Silence

Felicity Heathcote

The OtherWorld Press

©2024 Felicity Heathcote

Cover image © Heba Zagout

The moral rights of author have been asserted in accordance with the Act. All rights reserved. No part of this publication may be reproduced, stored in a retrieval system, or transmitted, in any form or by any means without the prior written permission of the publisher, nor may it be otherwise circulated in any form of binding or cover other than that in which it is published by this publisher and without a similar condition imposed on a subsequent purchaser.

This edition: Paperback
13-digit ISBN 9798883472793

Published by OtherWorld Press 2024
13-digit ISBN 9798883472793
A CIP catalogue record for this title is available from the British Library

The OtherWorld Press

Cover Design by Eoin Mulcahy
Front Cover Painting by Heba Zagout
Back Cover Illustration by Vic Lepejian

Contents

Preface

AMER'S STORY
By Seamus Cashman

PARADISE LOST
2006

THE WORLD MOVES ON
2008

A GAZA DIARY

Dec 27th 2008 — Jan 17th 2009

Epilogue

MISTRUTHS IN GAZA
By Dr. Niall Holohan

The author's royalties from the sale of this book will be used to provide humanitarian and medical aid to the most vulnerable people in Palestine.

Dedication

This diary is a record of some of the terrible sufferings of the people of Gaza over decades. Nothing has really changed since the winter of 2008/9 other than the scale of the death and destruction. At the time of writing, the numbers of dead and missing in 2023/4 have now risen to well over thirty thousand. The injuries, especially those of the children, are too unbearable to contemplate and there is still no end in sight, no sign yet of a ceasefire permanent or otherwise.

This book is in memory of our friends in Gaza:
Heba Zagout a wonderful young mother, artist and friend, whose painting graces the front cover of this book. She was crushed to death alongside two of her sons when her house was bombed on 15 October 2023 as part of Israel's immediate act of 'self-defence'. All her beautiful paintings of Gaza and Jerusalem were also destroyed.

Samir Aloul a man who devoted his life to helping children in a special needs centre in Gaza, children who had lost limbs in previous bombardments or suffered from other disabilities. He died on 17 October 2023 when his car was bombed on his way to find food for the children in the centre. His son was also badly injured with shrapnel in that attack. The centre, which had carried out such good work, was destroyed in January 2024. Samir's colleagues are trying to continue his work under very difficult circumstances.

The family of Yousef Shehada, manager of the Palestinian Special Olympics Team, who died of natural causes in 2022.

His wife, children and grandchildren were all killed when their house in Rafah was destroyed by aerial bombardment on 15 December 2023.

To all the doctors, paramedics, UNRWA aid workers and journalists who died while healing the wounded or attempting to spread the truth.

To the American peace activist Rachel Corrie who tried to prevent houses bring destroyed by standing in front of the bulldozers. She was crushed to death before the eyes of the world in 2002. Peace volunteer Tom Hurndell was shot and killed in 2002 when trying to protect a young child. Cameraman James Miller was also killed in 2002 by an Israeli tank while carrying a white flag. Their names will live on.

This book is also in memory of the multitudes of dead and missing, named and unknown, in all the wars in Gaza over the years.

Acknowledgments

A special thanks to Jaber Wishah of the Palestinian Centre for Human Rights (PCHR) who sent documented pictures and stories of Operation Cast Lead (2009) to me in Saudi Arabia during the 2012 bombardments in Gaza. A man so kind and gentle, a delight to be with and a wonderful advocate for peace and justice.

Thanks to Seamus Cashman for his wonderful poem on Gaza. A poet and publisher, who has always been such an inspiration for my work and who published in 2006 and 2010 two of my books which others found to be too hot to handle, maybe because they dealt with subjects that, at the time, could not be mentioned - Palestine and prisoners of conscience.

To Eoin Mulcahy, a great guitarist, without whose invaluable, creative and technical input this book could not have been published.

To Maysaa sister of artist Heba Zagout for permission to use her sister's painting on the front cover. A picture taken from the archives as her paintings were destroyed when her house was leveled to the ground in October 2023.
To Vic Lepejian of Jerusalem for his special painting of the sacred hoopoe bird.

To all the Jewish academics. political commentators and journalists who have greatly influenced my works over decades especially: Jeff Halper; Ilan Pappé; Uri Avnery; Amira Hass; Gideon Levy; Tania Reinhart; Angela Godfrey-Goldstein; Ronit Lentin; Dr. Ruchama Marton and Meir Baruchin.

To Stephen Heydt former Director of the UNRWA psycho-social programme in Gaza and Richard Cooke former UNRWA Director in the West Bank.

To my family whose love and support helped me to complete this diary. My husband Niall, my greatest support, whose amazing knowledge of the Middle East has been invaluable over the years and who has never been afraid to speak out against injustice. My daughter Clare, who has been working tirelessly for human rights in Palestine for many years, raising money and advocating for the voiceless children of the West Bank and especially Gaza. My son Andrew, whose creative support has always given me new ideas and whose drawing of tiny birds have illustrated my books on Palestine and, of course, my grandson Ciaran who has made me laugh even in the darkest of times.

To Patrick Duffy for his many insightful conversations.

Finally my thanks to all my friends, especially Mothers Against Genocide and those who purchase this book and thereby contribute to peace and the rebuilding of the shattered lives of children in Gaza.

Amer's Story - *A poem by Seamus Cashman*
GAZA CITY JANUARY 2009

Is there any reason not to believe me?
Any reason at all.
I say they killed me three times, those machines.
They just came and when my father opened the door, the bullet killed
    him. That was the first time I died.
I know many fathers who never died like that.

We were ordered out of the house.
I wanted to stay with my dead father's body.
One said: Get out or we will kill you too.
I understood that so I abandoned my father's body.
It was to be six days before they let me back - in this hot weather?
Machines have taken over their brains.

There was more to come. My little daughter died.
Farah, joy of the whole world,
breast-fed by her mother to give some comfort
as her intestines leak through bullet wounds.
May I ask why? Are there only machines?
That was the second time I died that day.

Sejah, my other daughter, and my brother Abdullah.
They were shot too. That they didn't die was not the bullets' truth.
    Fourteen hours and still wandering in open spaces, we were
    trying to hide.
Then they released the dogs.
They released dogs ... those machines did.

Someone offered iodine and bandages — but that was a day later
    and we still prisoners
They blindfolded and handcuffed me. Took me for five days. The
first three no water, no toilet.

They asked Where's Gilad? How would I know?
All I know are my dead and my living.
Later, we came home.
We came home later.

We looked for eight hours and couldn't find my father.
Then someone saw his foot
sticking out of cacti rubble and dirt.
No room in our house left undamaged.
The broken clock on a bullet-pocked wall silent
Fouad was now dead. Finally dead.

We can bury him now
that the machines are gone.

Who cares about the stolen money, phones, gold, jewellery, biscuits
    — anything of value in our home? Who cares.
My delivery van too — a burned-out shell beside the house. I looked
    around at the whole wide world, the ground, the sky.
That was the third time I died. That day.
Fouad, my father, Farah joy of the world, and me.

Is there any reason not to believe me?
-Any reason at all.

Seamus Cashman, a former teacher in Tanzania, transitioned to editing with Irish University Press before founding Wolfhound Press in 1974. His publishing ranged from fiction to children's books, including anthologies and cultural studies, while also reviving works of Irish writers from the early 20th century. Wolfhound Press thrived until 2001, earning numerous accolades and enriching Ireland's small press scene. Cashman's editing prowess led to him receiving the Reading Association of Ireland's Special Merit Award in 2005 for the children's anthology "Something Beginning with P". As an established poet, he conducted creative workshops and curated events like the Poetry Ireland annual 'Poemathon'. Cashman served as a judge at the International Mamilla Poetry Festival and became the first International Fellow at the Black Earth Institute. Born in Conna village, East Cork, he resides in north Dublin, drawing delight and inspiration from his grandsons, Conor and Tadhg.

Preface

DECADES OF DESTRUCTION

In November 1917 a private letter from British Foreign Secretary Arthur Balfour created the context for the Zionist dream to be realised. The letter was addressed to the head of Britain's Jewish community, Lord Rothschild. It promised the establishment of a national home in Palestine for the Jewish people. Regrettably it failed to consult with the Arab people who were already living there. It had no legal basis but was written in the hope of gaining support from Jewish financiers and scientists during the First World War. The British had of course no right to give away Palestine to anyone as it was not theirs to give but was, at that time, part of the Ottoman Empire - but they appeared to have no qualms about making empty promises out of self-interest. The following month, British forces under General Edmund Allenby conquered Jerusalem and Palestine came under British control. What had formerly been a meaningless promise could then be fulfilled. Ever since, Palestine has suffered horrendously as a direct result of decisions made at that time.

Antonio Guterres, the Secretary General of the United Nations, suggested that - although the attack by Hamas on Israeli citizens on October 7 2023 was an appalling act of terror - it did not 'happen in a vacuum'. He was by no means condoning the attack, just attempting to put it into context. For decades the people in Gaza have been imprisoned in a tiny strip of land with very few resources, little work opportunities, endemic poverty and an inability to leave Gaza (even to travel to the West Bank to see their relatives).

A Gaza Diary

Since the time I first lived in Jerusalem (2002-2006) there has been frequent shelling and bombing from the Israeli side into Gaza, accompanied by rocket attacks from Hamas and other militant groups into Israel. After each bombardment there were denials of wrong-doing from both sides. What always stood out over the years for me, however, was the way any rocket assault by the Palestinians was immediately called a terrorist attack while there was an unbelievable lack of willingness on the part of most Western governments to call the massive Israeli attacks on civilian areas as disproportionate, let alone as war crimes. For these governments, there invariably seems to be a distinction between state violence which is regarded as self-defence and the violence of individual groups which is not. The militant groups, whom some label as terrorists and others as freedom fighters, often feel that no-one will pay attention to their problems if they play by the rules. For the Palestinians this indeed has been true. If they are violent, the world punishes them. If they do nothing (i.e. behave themselves), the world forgets them and continues with endless rounds of often meaningless talks about the peace process or seemingly unattainable two-state solution. In recent years there has been no room left for a viable Palestinian state due to the proliferation of illegal Israeli settlements together with the building of a network of settler roads on which Palestinians cannot travel. Still, however, politicians in every country continue to promote the panacea of the two-state solution which remains a time-wasting exercise without a simultaneous commitment to dismantle the settlements. There can be little hope for change when settlements are continually being built on Palestinian land without protest from the rest of the world. What is urgently required now is a permanent ceasefire and a radical innovative solution which will enable the Palestinians to achieve the homeland which is rightfully theirs.

The background to the Cast Lead Operation in Gaza is interesting once again showing that events rarely happen 'in a vacuum'. Six months before the 2008\9 assault a ceasefire was negotiated between Israel and Hamas. Both sides agreed to stop hostilities across the border between Israel and Gaza which had been blocked since Hamas took control of Gaza in 2007. This agreement was disputed by Israel and the closure policy did not change. Then in November 2008 Israeli soldiers raided Gaza and killed six members of Hamas. At this stage the ceasefire broke down and on 27 December the Cast Lead assault began. It lasted for three weeks and the world said and did nothing, bringing shame on us all.

World governments are still refusing now in 2024 to call for a ceasefire in the latest horrendous assault on Gaza. They are not listening to the protests from their own people or the many brave Jewish voices across the world. Nothing has changed and Israel continues to be given a green light by certain countries to do whatever it wants to "defend itself". These same countries are perhaps beginning to feel that over thirty thousand dead and missing under the rubble (mostly women and children - not the Hamas leadership, which appears to be living comfortably in Beirut or the Gulf States), appalling civilian injuries and starvation, while trucks full of food and medicines are parked outside the Rafah Crossing, is maybe a step too far. It is too late, however. The genie has been let out of the bottle and Prime Minister Netanyahu and his War Cabinet are refusing to listen to anyone. The only way the world can get them to stop their murderous behaviour now is for the US to cut off its arms supplies - but that seems highly unlikely in an election year.

This diary is intended to show that the destruction of Gaza did not start on 7th October. It has been going on for decades and it must stop. Children are now dying of starvation and disease inside Gaza while hundreds of trucks are blocked from entering the Rafah crossing with desperately needed supplies of food and medicine.

Gaza is dying! Is the conscience of world governments dead too? Are we living in a world in which integrity and decency no longer prevail? If so, then sadly, time for all of us is running out.

Felicity Heathcote
March 2024

PARADISE LOST
Gaza August 2006

Idyllic Scene

Daylight was fading as fishing boats stretched in a straight line a few kilometres out along the glittering blue-black sea. On each boat a tiny lantern glowed and as the sunlight died, this string of lights was all that was visible on the Mediterranean Coast. I sat in silence on the patio of the lovely Moroccan-style Al-Deira Hotel, enveloped by the sense of peace and beauty which this idyllic scene evoked. Below on the beach a small boy cantered on a black horse along the golden sand at the edge of the sea. Others splashed and skidded happily in the white fringed, foaming waves which crashed against the shore. All around, families sipped freshly made strawberry juice and drank strong Arabic coffee.

Milk and Honey

Then it happened – suddenly everything changed - the staccato sound of guns followed by the dull thud of a missile shattering its target. This brought me back to reality. This scene was not the south of France; this was the Gaza Strip, one of the most highly populated places on earth. The ancient land of the Philistines which was formerly a land flowing with milk and honey was now a lawless prison. I looked uneasily across at my husband, Niall, who was visiting Gaza in his capacity as the Irish Representative to the Palestinian Authority in Ramallah. My daughter Clare looked startled. She was completing an internship with the UN before going back to study for a Master's degree in human rights at University College Dublin. The previous day Niall had held discussions with John Ging, Director of UNRWA operations, about the humanitarian situation in Gaza. John had informed us of the many deaths caused by Israeli missiles in the areas of Beit Hanoun and Beit Lahya. He also discussed the loss of electrical services due to the shortage of fuel supplies along with the bombing of Gaza's only electricity generating plant. I was particularly interested in this information as I was running seminars for the psychologists, social workers and teachers working with UNRWA in Gaza, Jerusalem and the West Bank; it was important to assess just how stressful the daily work situation was for them. This was a difficult time for everyone as continual bombardment from the Israeli missiles was causing massive destruction in this crowded strip of land. Psychologists and patients were all caught up in this high-stress environment with each one in need of coping methods.

Relative Safety

Once again the peaceful atmosphere was changing and it was getting dark, all of which added to the feeling of risk and danger. We decided it was time to return through the Erez crossing back to the relative safety of Jerusalem where we lived on the Mount of Olives. On our way out a rocket whizzed over our head and a missile coming from Israel landed in the corner of a nearby field. Returning home, we felt so sad about leaving everyone behind in such a dangerous situation. (The beautiful Al-Deira Hotel on Gaza's coast, with its lovely stonework and inside courtyards was destroyed in December 2023)

Gaza is Dying

I had been to Gaza many times. It was one of my favourite places and I had never been afraid before. Since the Israeli disengagement the previous summer (2005), however, the situation had deteriorated. What most people did not realise, was that although all the Israeli settlers were removed from Gaza that year, nearly twice as many had been resettled in the West Bank. Sadly, disengagement did not mean, as the Israeli government claimed, that Gaza was free of occupation; in fact the situation since this time had become worse than ever. The beautiful biblical land of the Canaanites was now dying slowly. The economy was squeezed out of it and many children were malnourished. Out in the road at the front of our hotel a young boy was selling chewing gum trying to support his family and sick father. Every time we came to Gaza we would bring him books and pens for school and money for food and medicines; but this time he was looking sadder than ever.

Psychological Damage

The physical rubble of demolished houses litters this once-proud land. The psychological damage, however, caused by the Israeli policy of targeted assassinations by land, sea and air is even more serious. This policy results in the killing of many innocent civilians and causes widespread terror. Gaza is now cut off from the rest of Palestine, and without permits no one can travel out of Erez to Israel or through Rafah to Egypt. There is little or no work in Gaza and now very few people are permitted to work in Israel. The borders, the sky and the sea are patrolled, so those fishing boats, that look so beautiful in the evening light, can only fish for a few kilometres out to sea. This is the curse of Occupation. There are few customers to buy their produce while delicious fresh strawberries going out of Gaza are also held up for long periods at the port crossing, often until they rot. Aid agencies do their best to get essential food and medical supplies in but often with great difficulty. On several occasions we have seen senior American aid workers humiliated and strip-searched at the Erez border. If that is freedom – then Gaza is free.

THE WORLD MOVES ON BUT NOTHING CHANGES
2008

Humiliation

That was 2006 but the same humiliation and violence and lack of access to humanitarian aid has continued despite the best efforts of UNRWA who look after nearly two million refugees in Gaza. Most western governments make significant contributions to UNRWA but Israel contributes nothing and often hampers its operations. This is despite the fact that legally as an occupying power it should take responsibility for the population subject to occupation. It does not, however, even use the word occupation.

Whenever any UN facilities are destroyed, other countries are forced to foot the bill. Why is the world too afraid to stand up to Israel? (The day after the International Court of Justice in the Hague issued its preliminary ruling under the Genocide Convention, the Israeli government accused a small group of UNRWA employees of being connected with the Hamas attack of 7th October. Several of the major donor countries immediately suspended their essential funding without waiting for an independent investigation to determine the truth of the matter. As yet Israel has given no hard evidence to support its accusation.)

Punitive Measures

The Israeli peace group Gush Shalom also underlines the point that Israel as occupier should take responsibility for Gaza, rather than relying upon the goodwill of other countries and aid agencies. It said in its report:

"For the last 14 months Israel has deliberately and consistently restricted the transfer of fuel into the Gaza Strip as part of the Cabinet decision from September 19, 2007 authorising punitive measures against the residents of Gaza. Instead of fulfilling its duty to provide the civil population with the necessary humanitarian products before launching the military campaign, the Israel forces drained the Gaza Strip of the fuel, food and equipment needed to cope with the severe results of the fighting."

This type of punitive behaviour has been in place for several years. The latest military campaign has just compounded the existing problems with its widespread programme of destruction, deaths and injuries.

DECEMBER 2008

Jerusalem and the West Bank

Niall and I returned to the West Bank at the beginning of December 2008 and the news at that time was all about armed settlers who were on the rampage attacking and killing Palestinians in Hebron. Despite warnings, we went with our Israeli friend Ezra to spend time with the Bedouin and 'cave people' in the south Hebron hills. The Bedouin are even more deprived than the cave people in that area and survive mostly on bread and tea - meat is a rare treat. The cave people are routinely attacked by settlers. Their sheep are stolen, their water poisoned and their children are harassed on the way to school. These people live in caves in the hills and the settlers are trying to take away the land and their basic dwellings. Ezra has tried for many years to help them. He buys food and has been on many occasions imprisoned in Israeli jails as a result of his humanitarian activities.

Broken Heart

On our return to East Jerusalem we went to the tent where the wife of Mohammed al-Kurd was sitting with her family and various human rights activists. She remained quietly dignified despite having been thrown out of her home and having just lost her husband to heart failure because of the eviction. A group of settlers had taken over her house and this the second time she had lost her home - the first time was in 1948.

The eminent Israeli journalist, Gideon Levy, has been documenting the plight of the Palestinians for many years in the newspaper Ha'aretz. This is how he described the al-Kurd family's situation on this occasion:

"The Israeli national flag flies high, defiant and arrogant over the Palestinian home in the Sheikh Jarrah neighbourhood of East Jerusalem. This flag never looked as repulsive as it does in the heart of this Palestinian neighbourhood, above the home of a Palestinian family that suddenly lost everything. The head of the house, Mohammed al-Kurd, died 11 days after the eviction. Now his widow lives in a tent."

- Gideon Levy, 'Ha'aretz

This particular eviction has received quite a lot of attention but many thousands go largely unnoticed by the world. While

I was in Jerusalem, I was told that some of the people of Gaza were hungry and consequently forced to eat grass. I could not verify this because I was no longer able to enter Gaza. Paradise was finally lost.

DAY 1

SAT 27ᵀᴴ DECEMBER 2008

Operation Cast Lead

"To understand how frightening it is to be a Gazan this morning, you need to have stood in that small slab of concrete by the Mediterranean and smelled the claustrophobia. The Gaza Strip is smaller than the Isle of Wight but it is crammed with 1.5 million people who can never leave. They live out their lives on top of each other, jobless and hungry, in vast, sagging tower blocks. From the top floor, you can often see the borders of their world: the Mediterranean and Israeli barbed wire. When bombs begin to fall – as they are doing now with more deadly force that at any time since 1967 – there is nowhere to hide."

– Johann Hari, journalist

The attack on Gaza has started. I hear this morning that the attack has been threatened for some time now but we hoped against hope it wouldn't occur. F-16 fighter planes are relentlessly attacking the tiny Gaza Strip. The people have already suffered so much.

The foremost Palestinian psychiatrist in Gaza describes the first few minutes of the onslaught:

"The news came over the telephone and the television. More than 200 people had been killed and even more wounded in less than 10 minutes. The numbers were climbing and the funeral scenes filled the TV screen. Apparently F-16s had dropped more than 100 tons of bombs on crowded Gaza and had hit more than 300 targets in one mission."

- Eyad El-Sarraj

Human Rights

This time the military operation is called Operation Cast Lead, based on a Hanukkah toy for children. The Israeli army have a different name for each new military operation in Gaza. Over the last few years the lyrical sounding Operation Rainbow and Operation Summer Rains have been utilised. Quite grotesque, such lovely names for such evil killing machines.

Over 200 people are reported to have been killed in the first few minutes. I think in despair of all our friends in Gaza. Yousef Shehada and his family, who live in Rafah refugee camp, which is the most dangerous part of Gaza at the current time. Yousef is confined to a wheelchair and is the head of the Palestinian Special Olympics team and was over in Dublin for the Special Olympics held there in 2003. (Yousef himself died in 2022 but his family home was razed to the ground in December 2023 killing 28 people, including his wife, children and grandchildren.) I think too of the well known Human Rights lawyer, Dr Raji Sourani, who with Jaber Wishah runs the Palestinian Centre for Human Rights (PCHR) in Gaza city. We have had some lively and interesting discussions with both these men over the years. Jaber's mother is an amazing woman; although in her eighties, she still holds a vigil every Friday in front of the Red Cross offices in solidarity with prisoners who have not yet been released, Jaber himself, spent fourteen years in prison and now works tirelessly for peace and justice. (Jaber sent the stories from the PCHR office when I rang him from Saudi Arabia in 2012. In October 2023, the PCHR office itself was bombed and all its documents destroyed. Some believe that it was deliberately targeted in order to eliminate all records of human rights abuses in Gaza. Shortly afterwards the house of Raji Sourani was also destroyed.)

Bread and Tomatoes

Many people are affected by the present (2008/9) attack on Gaza including Hannan, a young woman whom Clare and I originally met when her three year old daughter was receiving treatment for glaucoma at St. John's Hospital in Jerusalem. While she was in the hospital in 2004 with her daughter, her house in Gaza, was bombed and she was forced to live for some time in a tent eating nothing but bread and tomatoes. She then moved into a shack with several other family members and we went to visit her there. Hannan's daughter required frequent medical visits to Jerusalem but she has not been allowed to leave Gaza. We wonder how they both are. I thought too of the deaf school 'Atfaluna' in Gaza city where children and adults were taught different skills and made beautiful sophisticated crafts, including stunning pottery and exquisite hand-made embroidery. Several years ago the Israelis had sent jets over Gaza city and the sonic booms had caused widespread distress; the deaf people naturally did not hear any of it although they could not understand why their pottery and machines were constantly shattering! (In December 2023 I was very upset to hear that Atfaluna had been bombed, leaving just a shell of a building. The Israelis said they had made a mistake but their 'mistake' destroyed the lives of many vulnerable individuals who now have no shelter.) I also remember meeting in Gaza city a group of people with disabilities who set up a cooperative where they made beautiful embroidery and handcrafts in order to feed themselves and maintain their dignity. Since the closure of Gaza's borders, none of these groups are able to make much profit and can barely survive. Where are they now, those gently smiling people who had been so happy to meet foreigners again and to sell the products of their craftwork?

Flying Trash Cans

The news reports that a police initiation ceremony has been attacked by F-16 planes in Gaza City, many policemen were killed. I remember the famous flag shop in Gaza City that we used to visit whenever we visited. It sold all sorts of unusual and humorous items including puppets of Yasser Arafat and Saddam Hussein. The Palestinians are very resilient and it was really great fun to see all the quirky items.

The official numbers of dead are announced – two hundred and sixty Palestinians are killed by Israeli bombs and one Arab-Israeli killed in Ashkelon by a Hamas rocket. Israeli foreign minister, Tzipi Livni (looking cool as ice), states that the Israelis are not against the people of Gaza. That's good to know and I'm sure they'll be pleased to hear that, as they cower in terror listening to the roar of F-16s and Apache helicopters overhead. These same people of Gaza have been imprisoned in a tiny space, one of the most overpopulated places on earth, close to starvation for some years now. They have also withstood missile attacks over the years and targeted assassinations with the usual civilian killings or 'collateral damage' as we prefer to call it. The Qassam rockets of which we are constantly reminded are what one American aid-worker described as "flying trash cans" or "glorified fireworks." That means that if they hit you on the head you are in trouble but otherwise they don't cause too much damage. (The rockets have become more sophisticated over the years but still do not compare with Israeli missiles.) Of course it would be preferable if no rockets were fired at all but there is somewhat of an imbalance when the missiles that return can destroy whole neighbourhoods and we don't hear too much about that. Now the people of Gaza are also facing bombs from F-16s.

UN Veto

Obama remains silent as George Bush and Condoleezza Rice blame Hamas. In Britain, Gordon Brown says the rockets must be stopped and Israel must avoid harming civilians. There is not much hope of that in the massively over-populated Gaza Strip.

The statements from the UN are also not strong enough but unfortunately the UN is prevented from taking action by the US veto in the Secretary Council. Furthermore, no UN Security-General can be appointed without the approval of by the US. Not much hope there either.

THE AL ASHI FAMILY

(Official testimony from Palestinian Centre of Human Rights)

27th December 2008

On the morning of 27 December 2008, at approximately 11:30, Israeli F-16's targeted a Gaza police initiation ceremony being held in the forecourt of "Arafat City", a government complex located in Gaza City. The attack resulted in over 60 deaths and 150 injuries. This incident formed part of the wave of attacks which marked the commencement of Israel's 23 day offensive on the Gaza Strip codenamed "Operation Cast Lead". Amongst those killed was 33 year old Faris Al Ashi, a member of the Gaza police force who was on duty at the time of the attack.

Like many of the wives who lost husbands during the offensive, Amna Al Ashi was left with sole responsibility for bringing up her and her deceased husband's young children,

Khawla, 6, Osama, 5, Yomna, 3, and Faris, 2, whom she was five months pregnant with at the time of the attack. Amna's reaction to her challenging circumstances has been defiant, "I am a woman and I have the right to live my own life, many men have proposed but I choose to dedicate myself entirely to the cause of my children". Discussing the last three years of her life, Amna is keen to press upon the mini victories that have kept her going along the way.

It is clear that Amna has thought carefully about the solutions to the problems faced by her children following the loss of their father. "After he lost his father Osama was very traumatised", says Amna, "he didn't want to interact with others and he developed speech problems as a result. Even though he was very young I enrolled him in a local martial arts course. At first he didn't not want to go, but slowly he gained confidence and now he is an orange belt and has overcome a huge amount of his shyness". Likewise, Amna has found a novel means to allow her children to express their trauma. "I registered Osama and Khawla in a course for movie animation. Of course their movies are based around their lives and those of their siblings and reflect a lot of what they are thinking and feeling. The movies give me an insight into their problems and allow me to talk with them about it". She plans to enrol all the children in traditional Palestinian Dabka (Dance) classes to make sure they grow up strong and healthy.

Nevertheless, Faris' killing has left an empty space in the family life of the children and Amna . "My children see their cousins with their fathers, they hear them calling him "Baba" and they are deeply aware of the absence of a relationship with their own father" says Amna, "sometimes I try to make up for this by getting them to call me Baba, but it's not the same, they need the feeling only their father could give them". The loss of her husband has also led to feelings of loneliness and isolation for Amna. "During the day I am strong for the children but at night I become weak, I need the arms of Faris, I need everything he gave to me".

Amna describes the initial year after Faris's death as being the most traumatic. "At first I had huge trouble sleeping. The problem thankfully improved but I still find it difficult at times to sleep at night", says Amna. One way Amna has looked to keeping her outlook positive is to keep busy on projects and hobbies. "I want to keep myself busy with good goals for my life. Currently I'm busy setting up a Kindergarten, which I have already received funding for." "For the upcoming anniversary of the war, me and other women who lost husbands in the attack plan to give gifts to orphans who lost their fathers during the war. The gifts will be inscribed with the words "On this day you are the beloved ones of your mother". We want children to remember they still have their mothers and they will always love them".

During the offensive, Israel illegally classified members of the civilian police force as combatants: this classification constitutes a wilful violation of the principle of distinction, a key component of customary international law. Hamas is a multi-faceted organisation, exercising governmental control of the Gaza Strip. As an organisation, it cannot be considered an armed group. Rather, a distinction must be made between Hamas' armed and political/civil components. The Izz ad-Din al-Qassam Brigades are the military wing of the Hamas organisation, they are an armed group, and are considered combatants according to IHL. However, Hamas' political and civil wings are comprised of civilians, who are legally entitled to the protections associated with this status, provided they do not take an active part in hostilities. Civil police, and governmental officials cannot be considered combatants. Attacks intentionally directed against these individuals constitute wilful killing, a grave breach of the Geneva Conventions, and a violation of customary international law.

DAY 2
SUN 28ᵀᴴ DECEMBER 2008

I attend a lunch party but I'm not really in the mood, consumed by the thought that unnecessary violence has just been unleashed and I know from experience that once started it will take a long time to stop and many innocent people will be killed. As I arrive, the hostess immediately asks about the situation in Gaza but as I move around the room and try to see what ideas people have, I am met by the usual reaction. Most people murmur politely and move away – strange woman, doesn't she know it's Christmas. The financial situation seems to be of much more interest. There won't be any financial situation at all if we don't solve this problem I mutter darkly to myself. Even if no one gives a fig for ethics and the plight of the Palestinians wouldn't the thought of potential world wide terrorism or the start of a new World War stir some discussion? Silly me, does anyone really care? I find this very depressing but I suppose it is understandable as few people have seen the real story in Gaza and everyday issues seem much more pressing. More importantly few people realise that what is happening this time is a different issue. This is not just some sporadic incident, this is going to be a long lasting affair.

"If Israel is allowed to continue hammering on Arab civilian populations in the name of "self-defence", organisations like Hamas and Hezbollah will continue to find recruits, resort to desperate measures and thrive. And be advised, Israel will be the catalyst for a third world war: not Iran, not the United States, not Russia, not China, not even Pakistan and India. Israel. However, we'll all be pulled into the abyss and Israel will not survive. World War II will look like a football skirmish in comparison."

- Tom Chartier

Horrific Injuries

My daughter phones Ramallah where she is working with the human rights organisation Addameer. This organisation advocates on behalf of prisoners and their families. Clare has just finished her thesis on 'The Right to Education for Palestinian Child detainees in Israeli Jails' which is a heart rending study of child imprisonment and torture. Her colleagues told her that the people in Ramallah are in tears watching the Arabic Al-Jazeera television; graphic pictures are shown on that channel of adults and children with limbs missing and other horrific injuries. The bodies of two young girls have just been pulled from the rubble and the news is breaking of five sisters killed in their bedroom aged 4 to 17 years.

The journalists seem a little less deferential to the Israelis than normal. In the past they seemed not to know all the intricacies of this complex situation and the robot-like approach of Israeli government and army spokespeople seemed to deter them "as like all politicians" they were extremely economical with the truth. We are only hearing news from Israel about the many rockets sent from Gaza but I hear later this is because the Israelis are not letting journalists into Gaza so they are only reporting from way outside Gaza with very little knowledge of what is happening on the ground.

Crushed Buildings

There are some pictures of F-16s, crushed buildings and huge columns of dark smoke rising. When I was in Gaza in August 2006 at the Erez crossing, a Qassam rocket left Gaza and a massive Israeli missile returned. On that occasion there had been many casualties during the previous few weeks and everyone was very scared. I had been living in Tehran many years ago during the Iran-Iraq war, under missile fire from Baghdad, these incidents were very frightening and after four weeks of bombing night and day I felt as if I was going crazy. There is however, a distinction between the relatively few Iraqi missiles that we faced in Iran and the massive and frequent F-16 bombings being carried out in Gaza. Night pictures of Gaza show continuous bombing – how terrified all the people must be especially the children who do not understand what is going on. (In 2023/4 the massive bombardment of Gaza, the displacement of civilians from the north to the south and the subsequent bombing of them when they arrive at a designated 'safe' place - such as Khan Younis, which is now nearly totally destroyed - has led to the traumatisation of the whole population of Gaza. There is now no safe place in Gaza. The Israel Defence Minister, Yoav Gallant said at the beginning of February 2024 that once they had finished with Khan Younis they will start on another designated safe space - Rafah. If that happens the only place to flee to will be the Buffer Zone between Gaza and Egypt. Is this the plan, the end of Gaza for Palestinians? It is certainly beginning to look like that and again and again the world stays silent.)

THE ABU TAIMA FAMILY

(Official testimony from Palestinian Centre of Human Rights)

"Living under occupation means that whatever hopes we have, it will fall apart one day. For example, you bring up your child and put all of your hopes in him or her, but then they come and kill your child and all your hopes are destroyed."

28th December 2008

In the early morning of 28 December 2008 Mahmoud Abu Taima, his wife Manal, and their two oldest sons, Khalil and Nabil were collecting zucchini from their lands in Khuza'a village, east of Khan Younis. After a few hours the two brothers went to their uncle's farmland a few hundred meters further west. At around 8:30 the Israeli army fired a shell from the border fence which landed between the two boys. Nabil (16) was killed and Khalil was critically injured.

"You must understand, the area was very calm. Many farmers were working on their lands. It is an open area. I saw a projectile coming from the border fence towards the farm lands. Then I heard the explosion. I immediately ran towards the place of impact because I knew my sons were in that area. By the time that I arrived, people had already put the boys on a donkey cart to bring them to the hospital," recalls Mahmoud Abu Taima (40). Khalil was critically injured by shrapnel in the chest and limbs and underwent a life saving surgery immediately after arriving in the hospital. "While we buried Nabil we were expecting that they would bring Khalil's body from the hospital too," says the boys' mother Manal (37).

The Abu Taima family, who have their home in Abasan village, east of Khan Yunis, has been traumatized by the death of their son and brother Nabil. His parents, and 6 siblings Khalil (20), Naima (18), Isra' (15), Mohammed (14), Abdel Rahman (9), and Ibrahim (6) all have dear memories of him. "Nabil was a part of us and he had a big place in my heart. I remember him in every moment and I feel that he is present with us. Like now, when I drink tea, I remember him and feel that he is present. When I eat my meals I feel as if he is still here with us. I can never forget him," says his father Mahmoud.

"Nabil's mind was older than his age," says Manal, "he was very clever at school and all of his teachers and the students liked him a lot. On the anniversary date of his death, his teachers and friends come to visit us. Besides going to school, Nabil liked to breed rabbits. Until his death we had about 50 rabbits. Since his death they died and we stopped getting new ones. We don't feel like it anymore, now that he is not here."

Ibrahim (6) and Abdel Rahman(9) had a very close relationship with Nabil. Manal says: "They were badly affected by his death. They wanted to take the shovel and open his grave so they could take him from his grave and bring him to a doctor for treatment. Ibrahim was upset and stressed for a long time so I took him to a psychologist. When I told the children that a human rights organization was coming to talk to us Ibrahim asked me if they would bring Nabil."

Khalil has spent the past years trying to recover from his physical injuries. "After 3 days I was transferred to Egypt for additional surgery. In the months after that I went to Médicines sans Frontières after finishing school and had 3 hour sessions of physiotherapy. I had very long days. Despite everything, there is still shrapnel inside my legs, chest and arms which cannot be removed. There are places in my left leg in which I can't feel anything. My ankles always hurt and I can't move the way I did before. My mobility, including my walking, has been affected. I can't do everything that I want. For example, nowadays I play football alone because I am too afraid someone will hit my leg and I will be in agony."

Besides his physical injuries, Khalil is trying to deal with the loss of his brother and the trauma of the incident. "We would always go to school and other places together. I feel as if I lost a part of my body. It is difficult to continue my life without this part. During the war it was my 'tawjihi'[final high school] year and I had to go to school. I was traumatized after the incident. When I was sleeping I could hear the sound of a missile coming towards me. Somehow, I passed the tawjihi that year and am in university now." Manal adds that Khalil used to have panic attacks after the incident, "even the sound of birds could make him have a panic attack."

A few days after the attack, Israeli bulldozers destroyed the farmland belonging to the Abu Taima family, approximately 700 meters away from the fence. "We had zucchini crops, and a small storage room for fertilizers and equipment. We also had a water pump and water irrigation network. It is all destroyed now. We were unable to go to our farm for 2 years as it was too dangerous. Now we go again, despite the Israeli army shooting towards us. It is difficult. Since the death of my son I lost my motivation to work in the land," says Mahmoud.

The family is not optimistic of the chances that they will see a court case against those responsible for their son's death. "Nabil was not the first and last one who was killed by the army. Many boys like him were killed. Even if they [Israel] can capture the soldier who fired the shell, they will say he is insane," says Mahmoud.

DAY 3

MON 29TH DECEMBER 2008

I phoned my editor, the Irish poet Seamus Cashman, he and his family came to stay with us in Jerusalem in 2005. Now as they watch the current situation in Gaza on the television they are as horrified as I am. After his stay with us Seamus wrote several poems on Palestine and was asked to be a judge at the Festival of Poetry in Ramallah. He and I discussed how Israel had clearly been breaching the human rights clauses of its Association Agreement with the EU. Despite all the evidence readily available, no action has ever been taken by the EU to demand that Israel meets its commitments under these clauses. (It is only since the ruling by the International Court of Justice in the Hague in 2024 on the plausibility of genocidal actions by Israel that the Irish Taoiseach Leo Varadkar has stated that the EU-Israel Association Agreement should now finally be called into question.)

Any country which can unilaterally bomb a civilian population should be held to task. Tanks and bulldozers are lining up on the border for land invasions: aren't they already doing too much damage and killing enough innocent people? (In February 2024 more than one million people are living in flimsy tents in the wet and freezing cold in Rafah, terrified while waiting for another land invasion. If this happens there will be a total massacre of innocent people.)

Picnic on the Beach

Now they are attacking Gaza from the sea, the beautiful deep turquoise sea that borders the ancient land of the Philistines. Several years ago a Gaza family was bombed by Israeli gunships while picnicking on the beach. Pictures were shown of a 12 year old girl running down the beach screaming for her family but the family was dead. The Israelis accused the family of being blown up by their own missile. Human rights groups denied this and said they were bombed from the sea. A big fuss was made of this child at the time, the young girl was going to be adopted and looked after by a prominent Palestinian politician. Nothing happened and a few weeks later she was found in a room staring at a wall. Psychologist Stephen Heydt who ran the UNRWA psycho-social programme in Palestine worked with her and other children like her. A brilliant psychologist, he really cared about his work and his input in the UN was very effective. When he left Gaza, however, I don't know what happened to these children. This is the problem for most of the people who are affected physically and psychologically by the ongoing trauma. The damage is too extensive so there is little or no treatment for the vast majority of people. As long as the brutal Occupation is continued, there can be no peace and consequently no peace of mind, however much treatment is available.

Humiliation Tactics

Stephen asked me to train the psychologists and social workers for UNRWA in Gaza, helping them to cope both with their own stress and to help them learn techniques from which the traumatised population could benefit. I carried out seminars and workshops in the main UNWRA building (bombed in 2023) but my visits were restricted due to the closures of Gaza and the exchange of rockets and missiles. Niall always drove our car into Gaza because Palestinian drivers were not allowed in through the Erez checkpoint and each visitor was subjected to delays and searches. Our diplomatic car was checked for explosives by dogs. This was a meaningless gesture which was really just a humiliation tactic. An American aid worker was regularly strip-searched at the border presumably because he was taking aid to Palestinians. Senior UN officials and diplomats were routinely hassled by arrogant, young Israeli Defence Force personnel. For the Palestinians of course, it was another matter – it was often a case of life or death. Belongings were scattered all over the ground in a so-called search, people were dying at checkpoints. Some Palestinians were left lying for long stretches in the sun and cancer and heart patients were refused entry into Israel for medical treatment even if they had Israeli permission and the correct papers. I was always happy to see that Niall was very strong with his arguments and would not let the Israeli soldiers get away with any unfair behaviour. Clare and I would also take on the IDF when we saw them abusing Palestinians who were blindfolded and crouching painfully for long periods in the hot sun. To our amazement on many occasions this worked: we embarrassed the soldiers who always liked to be seen as the 'good guys'.

All of that is immaterial now, however, as I sit in Ireland and hear of the bombing from air and sea while everyone waits in fear for a possible land invasion of this tiny beleaguered Gaza Strip. (At the end of February 2024 there is a similar situation in Gaza as the world waits in horror for a threatened land invasion in Rafah which is packed with more that a million people.)

Coordinated protests are starting all over the world – that is really good but the silence of governments particularly in Europe and the US is truly deafening. (Fifteen years later, nothing has changed.)

ANWAR BALOUSHA & SON MUHAMMED

(Official testimony from Palestinian Centre of Human Rights)

"I miss them all the time, sometimes I even go to look for one of them in the house in the split second before I remember they were killed"

29th December 2008

At around 00:00 of 29 December 2008 an Israeli aircraft attacked the Imad Akel Mosque situated in Jabaliya refugee camp. The attack destroyed the home of Anwar and Samira Balousha, which was situated just three metres from the mosque. Five of the family's eight daughters were killed as a result of the bombing, which caused the family home to collapse on top of them as they slept. Five others were injured in the incident and other homes in close proximity to the mosque were completely destroyed.

In the main room of the reconstructed Balousha family household stands a portrait of the family's five deceased daughters Tahreer, Ikram, Samar, Dina and Jawaher who were 18, 15, 13, 8 and 4 respectively at the time an Israeli F-16 dropped a bomb on the Imad Akel Mosque, 3 metres from the family home. The family have since welcomed one new comer to the family, Tahrir (named after her deceased sister); but for father Anwar "the home still feels empty, it is like there is gaping hole where my daughters once were, and despite feeling their presence with us all the time there is a huge sense there is something missing".

While his face and composure gives little away in terms of the suffering his family has gone through, Anwar's words are clear regarding the effect the incident had on himself and his family. "My wife has been badly affected, just yesterday there was an UNRWA crew demolishing the wreckage of one the neighbours' homes destroyed in the war to make room for its reconstruction, it reminded Samira of the war and she started to cry". Anwar himself says he spends a lot of time at the daughter's graves talking to them about daily life's small comings and goings, "I miss them all the time, sometimes I even go to look for one of them in the house in the split second before I remember they were killed".

The family's remaining children have been traumatised. Anwar describes how Iman, 20 , who had a very close relationship with her older sister, Tahrir, and who watched her sister Dina die in her arms following the attack, seems often to be lost in her own thoughts; "sometimes I call her but she cannot even hear me" says Anwar. Despite being very intelligent Iman's grades have suffered as a result. He also fears that his son, Muhammad, who was recently treated for a shrapnel wound in his foot, suffered during the attack, will grow up wracked by feelings of revenge for the death of his sisters. "He speaks of them constantly", says Anwar, "he will not forget". When asked by his father about his sisters, Muhammad says that "my sisters were murdered by the Israeli's, they are in Paradise".

The three years since the attack has been a period of constant flux and displacement for the family. They have had to move home seven times in the past three years, each time creating a greater sense of instability for the family's remaining children. "The children find themselves friendless each time they move area", says Anwar, "my son Muhammad wanders off back to the neighbourhood of his old homes or to the local UNRWA school in search of friends, we can't find him for hours and when he eventually comes home he says he went to find friends to play with". They have only recently returned to their rebuilt home that was destroyed during the attack.

Regarding hopes and fears for the future Anwar has mixed feelings. He is hopeful for the family's legal case in Israel but he says "if they bring me all the money in the world they could not compensate me, I want my daughters, not money". He is ravaged by fear for his children every time there is bombing and fears that he will lose them in the future. "Though this is my home I am seeking a future outside Gaza, right now I want to leave to make a new life for me and my family".

PCHR submitted a criminal complaint to the Israeli authorities on behalf of the Balousha family on 2 August 2009. To-date, no response has been received.

DAY 4
TUES 30ᵀᴴ DECEMBER 2008

Attacks are continuing. I hear from friends in the West Bank who are very upset watching the images on Al-Jazeera. If people in Europe and America were forced to watch news coverage on Al-Jazeera it might be a very different story. Two more girls aged 8 and 10 years are pulled out of the rubble. Two boys are shot dead in Bil'in during the peaceful demonstrations for Gaza. I didn't hear too much about that on our news channels. Angry demonstrations are held in Iran, Lebanon, Turkey and all the Arab world. Have we no sense? When will we realise the effect our silence and partisan behaviour is having?

Missile Fire

Three more Israelis were killed yesterday, and there were some reports of friendly fire. One Israeli is treated for hysteria. There are also reports of three hundred and sixty to four hundred and fifty dead in Gaza. Are they all Hamas? The psychological trauma of qassams is horrifying and should not happen but the lack of balance in the conflict is also horrifying and the numbers prove this. Israel is complaining that the world is silent when the rockets have been coming from Gaza – that is incorrect – all we seem to hear about is rockets and we have done so for years. In the past we have not seen or heard about the returning missile fire. Based on this, it seems one Israeli life is worth more than hundreds of Palestinian lives. The world governments even refused to use the word 'disproportionate' when Israel destroyed Lebanon two years ago. I was living in Jerusalem at the time and couldn't believe that so-called civilised governments were allowing this to happen, without even calling for a ceasefire.

Why Now?
The question being asked is why now? This attack has been threatened for a long time and rarely does Israel make idle threats, so maybe the answer is why not now? Some journalists covering the conflict, however, are quite cynical about the reason for the attacks at this time. They suggest it may be because of the forthcoming Israeli elections. It is necessary for the politicians to be hawkish because Olmert is resigning and there will be a battle between Netanyahu, Barak and Tzipi Livni in an attempt to replace him. Another possible reason is the transition period in the US. As yet there is no real president in the White House and no one is quite sure how Obama will act after his inauguration. Sadly, however, his silence and his cabinet appointments may suggest that there won't be too many changes in America's Middle East policy which has already proved to be so disastrous..

Death all around
Clare texted Yousef Shehada and received back a chilling message, "we don't know what to do, there is death all around, please help us." I spoke to him on the phone, he sounded very frail but delighted to hear from the outside world. We met

Yousef many times in Gaza. Sometimes he would drive up to Gaza city to meet us in the Al-Deira Hotel beside the sea and several times we went down to the Rafah refugee camp to see his work with children with disabilities. He also ran summer camps for children, a great idea for those who have nothing to do and nowhere to go in an overcrowded refugee camp. These were payed for by the Irish and other EU Governments. If we really want peace, these are the sorts of activities we should be encouraging. Like all Palestinians, Yousef was very hospitable and invited us to meet his family for lunch in his house. He showed us the bullet holes which had come through the outside wall and narrowly missed his wife who was cooking in the kitchen in one of the earlier Israeli offensives.

Special Olympics

When I first met him he told me how on the way to Ireland for the Special Olympics, one member of the team was a 29 year old with a mental age of 9 years, he had been stopped at the Rafah crossing into Egypt and kept in the stifling heat for three days as the Israelis investigated whether or not he might be a security risk. Finally after three days waiting in the burning sun they decided he wasn't a risk and said he was allowed to leave for Ireland. Unfortunately they would not let out his helper and as the team had already left he was unable to travel to Ireland. This is an example of the cruel restrictions and of the humiliating behaviour imposed daily on the Palestinians.

Please help us

When I phoned Yousef, he said he had received a phone call earlier telling him to leave his house because the Israelis intended to destroy the whole area. Where can he go? The whole of Gaza is being targeted. Yousef lives in the Philadelphia triangle near the Rafah tunnels, these tunnels are suspected by the Israelis of smuggling weapons from Egypt. This might be happening, although no one has admitted that to me. I do, however, know that they are used to smuggling food and blankets to help families to keep warm in the cruel Gaza winter. The blockade has gone on for years and the people have no other way of obtaining sufficient supplies.

"Please help us" Yousef kept saying, in tears I replied how sorry I was and how I couldn't do anything but write about it and I didn't know what to say to him. I was so ashamed as a European that no one was doing anything about the situation just as years ago no one had done anything about the situation of the Jewish people in Germany.

No Money, Little Food

Yousef just repeated he did not know what to do, he had nowhere to go, some people had moved into schools. He tried to get money from the bank but the banks have no money and they told him that no one's salary was being paid at the moment. He was trying to get food but there was no car available to take him anywhere and there was very little food in the shops.

I feel so helpless and so upset at the thought of Yousef sitting in a wheelchair in a house riddled with bullet holes, not knowing what to do while waiting in fear for an Israeli bomb attack at any time.

I remember the summer of 2006, standing in a supermarket in Ramallah watching the Al-Jazeera television pictures of burnt children in Lebanon. The allegation was of the use of phosphorus bombs. We saw desperate pictures that we are not shown on our TV screens. Even when we are shown a few distressing pictures, it is felt necessary to issue a warning on behalf of our sensitive Western natures that some viewers might be distressed by some of the images. There are many arguments for and against the use of graphic pictures. I personally can't bear to watch these pictures but at least I do know quite well what is happening because of my access to many sources of information. If I wasn't aware of the true story I surely would want to be told.

Selling Weapons

In the West we don't mind selling weapons to cause these injuries – good for jobs – but we are not so happy to see the result.

That day in 2006 I stumbled around the shop after seeing the images, blinded by tears feeling ashamed and helpless. How would I have felt if alive at the time of the Holocaust knowing that the majority of the world governments and church leaders were silent. The Jewish people suffered because the world was silent and now the Palestinians also suffer and the world still remains silent. Gideon Levy, a respected journalist for Ha'aretz, told me that he considered that he was only writing for the archives about the suffering of the Palestinians because most people did not seem to want to know the truth. Years ago people said they had not known about the Holocaust and he is now writing so that doesn't happen in the case of the Palestinians. In years to come people can no longer say that they did not know.

The Arab League and the EU are trying peace initiatives, a forty-eight hour truce has been called. The news reports that one rocket has reached farther into Israel, as far as Be'er Sheva.

THE HAMDAN FAMILY

(Official testimony from Palestinian Centre of Human Rights)

"When I wake in the morning the first thing I do is remember my children. I come and sit outside and picture them where they used to play. I don't want to go out and interact with other people anymore. I largely stay inside the home"

30th December 2008

Talal Hamdan, 47, and Iman Hamdan, 46, are quietly contemplative about life since the loss of their three children Haya, Lama, and Ismail. The children were aged 12, 10, and 5 respectively, when on the morning of 30 December 2008 an Israeli F-16 dropped a bomb in the area they were walking in Beit Hanoun, killing all three. The children were walking with their father to a nearby rubbish site to drop off household waste when Israeli forces targeted the area. The children were the youngest of the couple's children, and they have not had any other children since the attack.

Though none of the previous three years have been easy on the couple, for Iman the hardest period was directly after the attack, when she found herself in deep shock. "After the death of my children I could not cry, I did not have the space to properly mourn them," says Iman, "but when I finally became alone. I couldn't stop my tears." Iman believes the shock of the incident has greatly increased her physical health problems, which include severe back and leg pain. "I barely sleep at night, maybe two hours during the day," says Iman. Her grief is compounded by the experience of losing her father, brother and two cousins all on the same day during the first intifada.

Talal's life has also been completely changed since the death of his children. "When I wake in the morning the first thing I do is remember my children. I come and sit outside and picture them where they used to play," says Talal. "I don't want to go out and interact with other people anymore. I largely stay inside the home." Talal had a very close relationship with Ismail, "he would beg me to take him everywhere with me and so I would take him, we were always together." Relating how the memory of his children is so painful, he gives an example of the time he was sick and needed to go to the hospital, "this particular hospital was the one the children were transferred to before they died. When I walked in the memory of my three children lying dead next to each other came back to me and I started to cry. The doctors first thought I was afraid of injections, my family had to explain to them what had taken place, and why I was so upset. In the end I couldn't stay in the hospital for the treatment."

Contemplating the approach of the upcoming anniversary, the couple speak about how they will face it. "On the day of the anniversary I will try to keep myself busy to avoid thinking about it too much" says Iman, "but I don't visit the graves, I couldn't bear it". The couple now have young grandchildren living with them, one of whom is named Ismail after their killed son. "We try our best to make up for our loss with Ismail, we go up and see him and spend time with him every morning," says Talal.

Before the attack Talal had worked in construction. He tried to return to work after the attack, but nerve damage in his legs and arms as a result of the attack have left him unable to continue working. The family now survive on UN food aid and help from their two sons.

Regarding the future the family has hopes and apprehensions. "We are always afraid that an attack will take place again resulting in more deaths in the family. I am always calling my daughters to tell them to take care of themselves and the children" says Talal. "I hope that peace will prevail and that we will return to calm eventually. Most of all I hope that other children are not killed in similar incidents. I can understand when adults are killed during war but I cannot understand when children are killed." Regarding the family's legal complaint following the death of their children, Talal is positive. "I expect it to be successful, my children were not militant and there were no military targets in the proximity."

PCHR submitted a criminal complaint to the Israeli authorities on behalf of the Hamdan Family on 21 July 2009. To-date, no response has been received.

DAY 5

WED 31ST DECEMBER

Israel refuses the EU plan of an immediate Gaza truce and say they plan to go ahead with attacks against Hamas.

Today there is some relief in Gaza at last. Bad weather is causing fewer air strikes to be carried out because there is too much cloud. That is good news but they are bombing the tunnels, I hope Yousef is safe.

Jaber Wishah emails an article telling us that his cousin's house has been destroyed by bombs while the family were inside and that the five girls killed on Monday were also members of his family. Johann Hari writes an excellent article discussing how Israel's actions are harming themselves.

That is so true, the Israeli soldiers who formed the group called 'Breaking Silence' told me how they were traumatised by their actions in the West Bank, particularly in Hebron. They were depressed, had sleepless nights and terrible nightmares. They were ashamed to tell their families what they had done to Palestinians in the West Bank. There are no winners in a conflict like this, in fact there are no winners in any attempt at a military solution, as we can see from Afghanistan and Iraq. The only way forward in any peace process is through justice, dialogue and negotiation.

Immediate Talks

The Arab League calls for immediate talks between Hamas and Fatah. This at last is a sensible suggestion. There can be very little hope for peace in Palestine if the Palestinians continue to be divided. Hamas was formed with Israeli support in the late 1980s. It was formed because Israel did not want to have to deal with Yasser Arafat and the PLO. It was carefully nurtured by Israel as an alternative to the PLO even though Yasser Arafat was the first Palestinian leader to recognise Israel. This fact, however, was not readily acknowledged. In later years Israel often refused to dialogue with Arafat and his appointed prime ministers Abu Alah and Abu Mazen. This continual lack of dialogue and cooperation continued even after Arafat died and Abu Mazen became president. Abu Mazen was made to look like a helpless puppet of both the Americans and the Israelis; no improvement in the situation was forthcoming. Consequently, partly as a result of any real progress in the post-Oslo negotiations, Hamas was voted by a disappointed and disillusioned people to be the largest party in the Palestine National Council elected in January 2006.

The Wrong Democracy

I was there at the time of the elections and the results were regarded by most Palestinians as a shock. Many had been making a personal protest against the ineffectual government of Abu Mazen's Fatah party which was seen as subservient to both America and Israel. Perhaps they did not realise what would happen if everyone made a personal protest. Most people were very ambivalent about the results at the time and felt the protest vote had backfired.

Instructions went out from European capital cities to all Western embassies not to deal with Hamas despite its electoral success. If peace really was on the agenda, then this was not a very logical move.

Civil War

Palestine now had a democratically elected parliament which was something that America and Israel had been demanding for years. Unfortunately, however, it was not the democracy those countries wanted. The message went out therefore to continue to ignore Hamas. Development aid for the Palestinian people was drastically reduced. The import and sales taxes which Israel collected on behalf of the Palestinian Authority were no longer transferred to Ramallah. Much of the money that European countries gave to the Palestinians as aid to pay the salaries of their policemen, teachers and nurses was cut off. For ten months these people received no money – no salaries. Most people continued working until they could no longer afford to pay for transport to work. The universities could not pay their staff and courses were stopped for months. Some people forfeited their degrees. Al Quds University was forced to borrow money from Jordan. Then the EU, following the American lead, had the bright idea of compounding the split even further by resuming money to Fatah in the West Bank but not to Hamas in Gaza. Even parents know that favouring one child over another causes major conflict and even worse behaviour in the family. The Palestinians are no angels, the two groups fought viciously, but it did seem as if the international community wanted civil war.

Peace

If the Palestinians want peace they must talk to each other and resolve the dispute and if world governments genuinely want peace they must talk to Hamas.

In the words of one commentator:

"The American and European are responding with lopsidedness that ignores these realities. They say that Israel cannot be expected to negotiate while under rocket fire, but they demand that the Palestinians do so under siege in Gaza and violent military occupation in the West Bank."

I ring Jaber Wisher. It's so nice to hear him, I congratulate him on his article and express my regret over the deaths in his family, he asks for all of us, saying how much he misses us. I gently remind him that we are the ones worried about him and his family in such a terrible situation. Jaber acknowledges the two things that worry him most are that the Israelis repeatedly bomb the same place and when people were taking bodies out of the rubble they bomb it again. Also he worries that the real war has only just begun.

Terrible Night

I phone Yousef again in the most dangerous place on earth, the Philadelphia Triangle in Rafah; he said it has been a terrible night. I tell him I saw that they had bombed the tunnels and left huge craters in the ground. He says he wanted to go out to get food but it was too dangerous. Eoin Murray who worked with Jaber and Raji for several years rings back to tell us Raji Serani is in Egypt. At least we don't have to worry about one person although I suspect his family is still in Gaza.

The hospitals are in a desperate state. There are shortages of everything, medicines, anesthetics, electricity. There are stories of operations done without anesthetics. (There are similar stories in 2023/4 except that so many hospitals have now been destroyed that there are barely any still functioning.)

Journalists are still not allowed into Gaza and everyone in the Arab world is watching Al-Jazeera. If Israeli actions are justified and carried out in accordance with international law, why are journalists not allowed into Gaza? (Journalists in 2023/4 have been allowed into Gaza but well over one hundred of them have been killed.)

Waste of Money

Britain offers to pour ten million pounds into Gaza. Unless there is a lasting peace and the Israelis are made accountable for their actions, this is likely to be a waste of money. Even under normal circumstances most of the money in Gaza is wasted because of the continual bombardment by Israeli missiles. A small port was built and a modern fishing boat was donated by the Danish government several years ago. The Israelis destroyed the port and imposed a fishing limit of several kilometres. The new facilities were rendered useless. The UN took us to visit a tile factory which had been one of the most successful family businesses in Gaza until it was bombed by the Israelis - on the usual pretext of security concerns. We walked among the ruins of the destroyed factory in which several workers had been killed. As the son of the owner showed us around he told us that his father had built this up from nothing and was so proud of its reputation as the best tile factory in Palestine. After the bombing he became severely depressed and left Gaza. Several people in our group wiped away tears as we heard the story told with quiet dignity by the young man. Another incidence of jobs lost and lives shattered. There are many more stories like that. If the Israelis agree not to destroy the Palestinian facilities built with EU money, then the aid is worthwhile. This ought to be the first step in any aid donation by a Western country.

Silence

Still the world is silent. When there is silence we are all complicit.

Israel held cabinet meetings to discuss the progress of their military not, unfortunately, to discuss a possible truce. They rejected the idea of a forty-eight hour truce in order to allow humanitarian aid into Gaza.

Yesterday the Israelis rammed the Free Gaza boat with a former American congresswoman aboard as well as doctors and medical supplies. The boat went to Lebanon. Given the ferocity of the Israeli bombing, they were probably some of the lucky ones. (In 2010 Israel refused to allow an Irish boat to bring in aid and killed 9 people on a Turkish aid boat. The Israeli Government seems to be able to do anything it wants.)

What is Tony Blair doing in all this as Middle East envoy of the Quartet? "Flapping about" in the words of one journalist. Blair is also saying that we can't talk to Hamas because that is Quartet policy. How can the world solve the problem if no one will talk to one of the groups? Surely governments can learn from the peace process in Northern Ireland.

We have a quiet New Year's Eve in Northern Ireland where my husband Niall is now working. We are all feeling very sad because of the happenings in Gaza.

THE ABU AREEDA FAMILY

(Official testimony from Palestinian Centre of Human Rights)

"Before my mother's death we used to be very happy on 1 January, have celebrations and visit people. Now we are all silent in the last hour of each year and on 1 January we don't celebrate the new year. We visit our mother's grave. We remember."

31st December 2008

Around 23:30 on 31 December 2008, an Israeli warplane fired a missile at Najma Parc, a small green strip in the main street of the residential al-Shaboura neighbourhood in Rafah, killing two civilians and injuring dozens of others. Iman Abu Areeda (34) was one of the two casualties, killed by a piece of shrapnel that penetrated her brain. Seven members of the extended Abu Areeda family who were also in the house at the time of the attack were mildly injured by shrapnel. The Abu Areeda family was displaced for several weeks after the attack as the external walls in the front side of the house were destroyed. The internal walls and furniture were also damaged.

It was about half an hour before midnight on 31 December when electricity in the area was cut. Iman went to cover her youngest son, Mohammed, who was sleeping in his room. As she was leaning over him, the missile hit a few dozen meters away from their family home. The shrapnel that came through the outer wall killed her. Iman left behind her husband Mahmoud Abu Areeda (now 39) and their 7 children: Majd (20), Randa (19), Basel (18), Hibba (14), Islam (12), Watan (9), and Mohammed (6).

"My mother died when I was 15 years old. It was the age that I needed her the most. I was in shock and I couldn't believe that she died. I still do not believe it. I felt like not going to school any longer but I pushed myself and kept going because I know she would have wanted me to do so," says Iman's second oldest son, Basel.

His siblings, Majd, Randa, Islam and Hibba have been badly affected psychologically by the death of their mother. Since the attack they prefer to be by themselves, isolated from the rest of their family. Randa, Islam and Hibba received psychological support from a local NGO to deal with their loss and the traumatic experience of the attack. After a while their family noticed they started to recover and were able to interact again with the people around them.

Iman's oldest son, Majd, says the past three years have been very difficult for his family. "We were all scattered after the death of my mother. I was alive but I didn't feel alive. It took me a long time to believe that she had died. I had a very close relationship with my mother as I was her eldest child."

Majd was in his final high school year when his mother was killed. "I didn't prepare for my exams as I was suffering a lot psychologically. I thought 'even if I pass my tawjihi [final exams] my mother is not here to be happy for me'. I failed my tawjihi. I hope I can redo it again and succeed. My mom wanted me to be an educated person, to get married and to take care of my siblings. I hope that I can live up to her wish."

His brother Basel also faced difficulties in finishing his high school exams successfully. "Before the death of my mother I used to get high scores but after her death my scores dropped. My tawjihi was a disaster but thanks to the help of my uncle, the brother of my mother, I made it and I am now in university. I'm studying journalism," says Basel, holding one of his notebooks.

Since he lost his mother, thinking of the future makes Majd anxious. "I am afraid of losing someone else who is close to me. Now my father is the closest one and I am afraid something will happen to him. After the death of my mother I feel like I have a dead heart. When I laugh I feel as if I do something wrong, I cannot laugh when my mother is dead."

Basel tries to look at the future with hope. The memory of his mother motivates him. "I think of the future quite a bit. I know my mother wanted the best for us so for the future I hope that I will be able to finish my study, find work, get married and to have a family and to be respected in the community. Nothing can compensate for my loss and sadness, having lost the most precious thing I hold in my heart, but I know what my mother wanted for us and that is what I will try to achieve."

PCHR submitted a criminal complaint to the Israeli authorities on behalf of the Abu Areeda family on 2 July 2009. To-date, no response has been recorded.

DAY 6
THURS 1ST JANUARY

I phoned Yousef to check he was still safe. He said last night was the worst of all; he has left his home today for his sister's house which is quite close.

B'tselem, the Israeli human rights group says that two days ago Hamas was wrongly accused of loading weapons onto a truck. The truck was bombed and found to be carrying oxygen canisters. Nine members of the family of the man who owned the workshop were killed.

There is also news that a senior Hamas figure is killed with his family including four children. Tzipi Livni is in France saying there is no need for a truce because there is no humanitarian crisis. Other voices say the crisis is dire.

Clare leaves for Ramallah tomorrow, I'm very worried as she is six months pregnant but she wants to return for another month to finish her administrative detention campaign. She is working as advocacy officer to try to improve the lot of prisoners in Gaza and the West Bank and is very passionate about her work. The issue of prisoners is an essential part of any peace process. Administrative detention means holding people in prison with no charge and no trial, sometimes for many years. This is similar to internment in Northern Ireland during the euphemistically termed 'Troubles'.

THE NASLA FAMILY

(Official testimony from Palestinian Centre of Human Rights)

"I wish that if our fate is to die, that we die together, I wouldn't want anybody left to have to bear this sort of pain"

1st January 2009

On 1 January 2009 at around 15:00, Israeli military planes targeted a water tower across from the home of the Nasla family in North Beit Lahiya. The family were making lunch when the first bomb hit. As the family were trying to escape the smoke filled house, a second and third bomb struck the area, killing Ayoun Nasla, 6, and M'uz Nasla, 2.

For Ayoun and M'uz's father, Jihad Nasla, the memory of what happened that day is especially distressing. "I found M'uz with his heart outside his chest and my daughter Ayoun with part of her skull missing and her brains spilt out," says Jihad. "It is the night time, when I used to tell M'uz the stories of Abraham to get him to sleep, and when I go to visit their graves, when I most vividly recall the incident". "I can no longer go into clothes shops to buy clothes for my children, I used to buy for three boys and two girl's; I can't bear to buy only for three", added Fatima, 42.

The children's mother, Fatima, has also given a lot of thought and attention to that fateful day. It is clear that she ruminates on the moments, days and years before the attack took place. "M'uz used to go to the balcony of the house every morning and say "good morning" to Majdal and Herbia, where our family is originally from, and every night he would say "good night." The day he was killed he had said good morning but he never got to say good night," says Fatima. "M'uz used to have a favourite resistance song he sang all the time, it reminds me so much of him anytime it is played, especially because it is played a lot on the anniversary of his death, which also happens to be the anniversary of one of the resistance groups. The title of the song is now written on his grave."

The family dynamic has been dramatically changed since the attack, a result of the stress they all share; the stress of one family member increases the anxiety of the others. "My wife now cries every day, I have to try and calm her down every time and this has become a source of conflict between us," says Jihad, to which Fatima adds: "I cry so often I feel my vision is now starting to be affected." The children's anxiety also feeds into the parent's anxiety. "If Zeid wakes up in the middle of the night, when it's dark, he starts to scream. I then wake up terrified something is happening" says Jihad. The anxiety of the children is plain both from their parents discussion of the changes they have gone through since the death of their siblings, and their reaction to the unhappy topic of the discussion. "Mu'tassam was very calm until the incident. But he has started to become violent. His grades have also been lightly affected" says Jihad.

PCHR submitted a criminal complaint to the Israeli authorities on 9 September 2009. To-date, no response has been received.

DAY 7
FRI 2ND JANUARY

Today is my son Andrew's 23rd birthday. We all set off early from Armagh for Dublin airport; it's quite cold but not so much frost as the rest of the week so the roads are quite easy. Our friends, Dr Nazih Eldin and his wife Mary, are at the airport with their daughter Soraya. She is going to work for six months with Sister Susan in Ein-Karem. Sister Susan does a great job running a hospital for children with severe disabilities. She also looks after children in Gaza. Soraya has worked there for some time and is very dedicated to her work. We see the girls board the Air France plane and Mary and I go for coffee while Nazih leaves for RTE to be interviewed on the Pat Kenny show. When Nazih leaves he also takes the car keys with him by mistake, leaving Mary stranded so after coffee we take her to the television studios. Nazih is going to be interviewed about his work in MAP – Medical Aid for Palestine.

We listen to the radio in the car. Myles Dungan was the interviewer on this occasion and did an excellent job. The head of UNRWA Karen Abu-Zayad talked of a crisis, affirming that there is definitely a humanitarian crisis despite the protestations of Livni. She forcefully refutes the claim that Hamas are storing food and not distributing it. She firmly states that UNRWA collects the aid, takes it to warehouses and distributes it; finally she asserts there is definitely not enough aid in Gaza.

Open Prison

The Israeli ambassador was on the radio to provide 'balance' although there is no such thing as 'balance' in this David and Goliath situation. He was very smooth and plausible but the facts stand. At the very least there is a need for an immediate truce to let the aid through because there is not enough food and medicines in Gaza and Hamas is not abusing the UNRWA system. After that there should be an attempt to establish the permanent peace process that the Palestinians want and need. It should be peace with justice and that does not mean starving people in an open prison such as Gaza. This is not about being pro-Palestinian and is definitely not about being anti-Israeli.

It is about being pro-justice.

"We know that the 1.5 million inhabitants of Gaza were being starved, as the U.N. Special Rapporteur on the right to food, had found that acute malnutrition in Gaza was on the same scale as in the poorest nations in the southern Sahara, more than half of all Palestinian families eating only one meal a day."

- Former President Jimmy Carter

The difference between the Palestinian situation and the rest of the world is that food is available but is not allowed into the Gaza Strip. Instead it is left to rot at the borders. Yesterday there was a picture in the Irish times of Israeli school children brought out to the border to look out over Gaza and watch the bombing. Sadly this is an abuse of childhood and certainly no way to encourage peace in the next generation.

Boycott

Ilan Pappé feels that if Israel doesn't change its ideology and actions it should be boycotted and subject to sanctions. He is one of the notable groups of Israeli academics that is not afraid to speak out.

"But I am not naïve. I know that even the killing of hundreds of innocent Palestinians would not be enough to produce such a shift in the Western public opinion; it is even more unlikely that the crimes committed in Gaza would move the European governments to change their policy towards Palestine."

(Well, we have definitely seen that analysis turn out to be correct in 2023/4.)

More children are dead in Gaza including three young brothers. I'm worried about Clare, there is a forty eight hour closure of the West Bank because of demonstrations. Sister Susan says Clare can stay in Ein-Karem until the closure is over. We promise Andrew that we'll celebrate his birthday tomorrow.

THE EYAD AL-ASTAL FAMILY

(Official testimony from Palestinian Centre of Human Rights)

"The second of January is no different from any other day. Every day and every minute feels like the moment when I lost my sons. In everything there is a memory of them. I miss them all the time."

2nd January 2009

On 2 January 2009 at around 14:30 an Israeli drone fired a missile at an open area in Qarara village, close to Khan Yunis. The missile struck and killed two brothers, Mohammed (12) and Abed Rabbo (9) al-Astal, and their cousin, Abdul Sattar Walid al-Astal (11) while they were playing and eating sugar canes in the land.

"I was at home when I heard an explosion that was close to our area. An Israeli drone was flying in the sky above us at that moment." Eyad al-Astal recalls. "Approximately ten minutes later, my brother Ibrahim (28) came to my house and told me that my two sons and their cousin were killed by an Israeli shell. I rapidly left the house and headed to the scene about 250 meters west of my house. There I saw a deep hole. Traces of blood and fragments of flesh were still there."

Eyad tries to describe what the life of his family is like without Mohammed and Abed Rabbo: "Our lives have been very difficult since they were killed. Every time I see another boy their age, I remember my sons. I still cannot look at their photos, it is too painful." He says; "I always feel like crying but I try not to. My wife, Jawaher, cries everyday but tries to hide her tears from me. She does not want to add salt to my wounds. My wife always wants to go to our sons' graves with her mother, but I don't. I only went once and don't want to go again. I can't face the sight of their graves."

Besides Mohammed and Abed Rabbo, Eyad and his wife have five daughters and two sons. Mohammed and Abed Rabbo were the oldest children and their siblings were either very young or not born yet at the time of their death. The youngest child was born one and a half years after the war and will have no memories at all. "When the children ask us where their brothers are we tell them that they were killed, martyred, and are in heaven now", says Eyad.

The memory of his sons is at the tip of Eyad's tongue. "My son Khaled looks exactly like his brother Mohammed and I often find myself saying 'Mohammed!' when I actually mean to call Khaled." In order to keep going, Eyad tries to stay busy all the time, finding some distraction by meeting people and working as a mason.

Since the death of his sons Eyad is tormented by worries and fears for the safety of his other children. Before the death of Mohammed and Abed Rabbo he allowed his children to go anywhere at anytime. Even when there were explosions and shooting was heard in the area. After the incident he became very afraid for his children and he wants to keep them inside. "I am afraid that anything would happen to them, especially for my son Khaled, who is now in the first grade. From the moment he leaves the house I worry that something could happen to him. Every day he walks to school, which is 1 kilometer away from our home. I know education is important, otherwise I would forbid him to go, out of my fear."

The children themselves are aware that their brothers were killed by a drone: the same type of drone they often hear and see flying above themselves. Eyad explains that "when they hear a drone they are too afraid to go outside. 'The drone will bomb me if I go out', is what they say."

The area where Mohammed and Abed Rabbo were killed was an open area approximately three kilometres away from the border with Israel. "The children were used to playing in that area. Our piece of land is close to it. It is an agricultural residential area, far from any hostilities," Eyad explains.

Eyad is sceptical about the future, given the continuing impunity. "The Israelis disregard our rights. They kill our children and bulldoze our lands and no one will hold them accountable," he says. "I expect the Israeli court to reject our complaint. I can even imagine them killing me together with my other children. However, I want to hope that the complaint would have some result."

PCHR submitted a criminal complaint to the Israeli authorities on behalf of the al-Astal family on 23 June 2009. To-date, no response has been received.

DAY 8
SAT 3ʳᴅ JANUARY

Ground forces go into Gaza at night. Unbelievable. How terrified everyone must be. The Israeli military machine is very frightening.

Bush in his address says that Hamas is to blame. Uri Avnery, one of the most impressive Jewish writers and activists whom I interviewed in Tel Aviv two years ago suggests that the "blood soaked moron could be expected to support the war enthusiastically as indeed he did." The Czech Republic, now taking over the Presidency of Europe makes a statement saying that Israel is engaged in a defensive action; the other countries of the EU had not, however, been consulted properly and there was uproar over this unilateral statement.

We take Andrew out for a birthday dinner with his friends but none of us are feeling like celebrating.

MOTEE' AND ISMA'IL AS-SELAWY

(Official testimony from Palestinian Centre of Human Rights)

"What affected us a lot psychologically is the fact that we were all praying in the mosque when we were attacked. The mosque is a place where we go when we need relief or when we are sad. We could never imagine them targeting us while we are praying in the mosque."

3rd January 2009

On 3 January 2009, at around 17:20, during prayer time, an Israeli drone fired a missile at the western entrance of al-Maqadma mosque in Jabaliya refugee camp. In the attack, 15 worshipers were killed and hundreds were injured.

"In every prayer I remember what happened in the mosque that day. I remember where I saw dismembered arms, legs and other body parts lying on the floor. I can still see our relatives and friends scattered around the praying room", says sheikh

Motee' as-Selawy (49) as he puts his head in his hands. He was standing on the sheikh's podium delivering a speech to the worshipers as the missile hit the entrance. "I had a direct line of sight to the door of the mosque and I saw pieces of red shrapnel flying towards us through the doorway," he recalls.

The extended as-Selawy family, who live together in one big house opposite the mosque, lost five of its members, all of whom were praying in the mosque when it was attacked: Ahmad Isma'il (22), Mohammed Mousa Isma'il (12), Ibrahim Mousa Aissa (44), Hani Mohammed (8), and 'Omar Abdel Hafez as-Selawy (27).

Motee's brother, Ismai'l Mousa as-Selawy (53), lost his oldest son, Ahmad Isma'il, in the attack. "I cry every day for my son. I have been suffering a lot over the past three years. He was everything for our family. I visit the grave of my son once or twice a week at least. I remember him in every moment, whether I am at home, in the mosque or somewhere else", says Isma'il.

"We miss our killed relatives on all occasions. Our family lives in the same building and we used to have a lot of fun together. Now we visit their graves", adds Motee'.

Six members of the as-Selawy family were injured in the attack and several of them continue to physically suffer from shrapnel that remains embedded in their bodies. "I still have shrapnel in my right wrist and it gives me problems until now. Doctors in Gaza said a surgery to remove the shrapnel might to do more harm than good. I feel constant tingling and my right hand is weak. I can't carry anything with it," says Motee'. Another relative, Mohammed Khalil es-Selawy (14), has shrapnel embedded in his head, which caused him to lose his hearing requiring him to wear hearing aids. Brothers Abdel Karim Mohammad as-Selawy (12) and Maher Mohammed as-Selawy (13) also have to learn how to live with shrapnel embedded in their bodies; Abdel Karim has fragments in his shoulder while Maher has pieces in his liver. Tamer Khalil (22) and Mousa Isma'il (23) as-Selawy were also injured by shrapnel in their backs but doctors were able to remove the metal parts from their bodies.

Motee' recalls, "Goldstone came to visit us in our house and went to the mosque with us to investigate. I asked him; 'where do you go when you feel sad and tired?' He said, 'I go to a place for prayer.' I asked him, 'what if you were bombed there?' Goldstone said; 'I cannot imagine it. Such a crime should be punished.' Now Goldstone has apologized for his report and we have not seen any results on the ground."

Since the attack the as-Selawy is not only mourning the loss of its relatives. The family members are also struggling financially as three of their deceased relatives used to provide for a vital part of the family income. Ibrahim left behind 9 daughters, who still live at home. "Who will take care of them now?" asks Motee'. 'Omar Abdel Hafez had 4 daughters and one son. Until the day of his death he earned the family income working as a cameraman with a local TV channel. Ismai'il's son, Ahmad, was the father of two children, Mohammed (5) and Nisreen (3.5), and used to work as a tailor.

"My concerns now are mainly focused on my grandchildren, Mohammed and Nisreen, and how I can bring them up. I want to give them a future but I am too sick too work. My health was badly affected by the attack and the loss of my son", says Isma'il, who suffers from severe migraine and stomach problems. "I try to take care of them as much as possible, but I will not be here forever".

The as-Selawy's try to deal with the financial difficulties by themselves as much as possible. "We have our dignity but we are forced sometimes to receive aid from people because we need to live" says Motee'. "Besides prosecution of the perpetrators, we need financial compensation to deal with our current situation."

The family has little expectations regarding the outcome of legal proceedings within the Israeli legal system. "The Israelis are prolonging the court proceedings and we don't see any positive results. We may have hopes if our case is taken to an international court," says Motee'.

PCHR submitted a criminal complaint to the Israeli authorities on behalf of the as-Selawy family on 2 July 2009. To-date, no response has been received.

DAY 9
SUN 4™ JANUARY

There are reports of bombing of a food market in Gaza city and the bombing of an apartment where children are playing on the roof. Calls from the UN for an immediate ceasefire are ignored. Five died and forty are injured in the market. An ambulance was hit and an Oxfam paramedic was killed.

In Ramallah, Clare is very upset as she tells me about a 6 year old boy lying on the floor of the hospital because there are not enough beds. He has a bullet in his mouth and his relatives are trying to resuscitate him but she sees him stop breathing and die on the television. All around him other patients lie on the floor as their relatives also try to resuscitate them.

A Norwegian doctor Gilbert working in al-Shifa hospital says that so far he has seen 2000 casualties of which fifty percent are women and children, he is one of the few Western doctors still in Gaza and he seem to be doing an amazing job.

Michael Martin (the Irish foreign minister) makes a good comment about the situation and gets criticised. Maybe such criticism is a badge of honour. Several years previously Brian Cowen as foreign minister chose to meet Yasser Arafat instead of Ariel Sharon as the Israeli government wouldn't let him speak to both parties. He was praised by the diplomatic corps in Jerusalem and Ramallah because, at the time, he was the first foreign minister to do this.

Dialogue

Thirty Palestinians died and one Israeli soldier was killed. Mahmoud Abbas pleads for the offensive to end but Israel is not listening.

Despite all the killing, Hamas is still sending rockets into Israel and causing a lot of psychological distress although very little physical injury. Dialogue is the only way.

Unfortunately the Israelis justify their defensive action as a reaction to more Qassam rockets hitting the town of Sderot. There is, however, no justification for such slaughter. Politicians in Britain call for an immediate ceasefire. Yesterday there were protests all over the world and the latest call for cessation of hostilities is vetoed in the Security Council.

Until there is a reform of procedures in the Security Council it is going to be difficult to achieve peace in the world.

I ring Jaber Wishah in Gaza and he says everything is really difficult but he thinks tonight will be the worst night yet. He asks for Clare's number in Ramallah so that he can contact her.

THE ABDEL DAYEM FAMILY

(Official testimony from Palestinian Centre of Human Rights)

"I was told initially that Arafa had been injured in an Israeli strike. Of course I was concerned, but many people get injured in his line of work and what was important is that he was still alive. I learnt only fifteen minutes before Arafa's body arrived back at the family home that he had died. The shock was unbearable"

4th January 2009

Arafa Abdel Dayem, 34, was killed on 4 January 2009, during Israel's 23 day offensive on the Gaza Strip, codenamed "Operation Cast Lead". Arafa, a medic, was responding to a missile attack on a group of five unarmed men when an Israeli tank fired a shell filled with flechettes directly at the group.

Meeting the al Dayem family one can't help but notice the quiet and composed nature of the whole group. It is obvious that the four boys: Hani, 11, Hamed, 9, Abdel Rahman, 6, and

Ahmed, 4, have been impeccably taught by their mother, Imtihan al Dayem, 35, in the ways of politeness and good behaviour. The boys remain quiet and seated next to Imtihan at all times during the interview.

The family have faced challenges since the loss of Arafa. Due to a dispute with Arafa's family, with whom they lived prior to the incident, Imtihan was forced to move out and into the unfinished house started by Arafa before he died. "When we moved in there was nothing, no furniture, no windows, no carpets, we only had the house painted ten days ago," says Imtihan. Using Arafa's savings she was able to pay off previous loans used to start construction on the house but did not have enough to finish it.

Reflecting on Arafa's life before he was killed Imtihan talks of Arafa's courage and popularity amongst Palestinians. "During the war, Arafa would only come home to deliver food to the family and then go out to volunteer with the medics again. If one medical crew was full he would look for others" says Imtihan. "We received condolences from all over the world when he died." Unsurprisingly, "the importance of being strong" is something that Imtihan reiterates in her discussion of the family's lives since the death of her husband.

The effect on the children on the loss of their father was particularly traumatic, especially Hani who, given his and his Dad's close relationship, displayed physical and mental symptoms of extreme trauma in the year following the event. "But I have been upfront with the children that they will behave as their father would wish them to," says Imtihan, and daily talking sessions with UNRWA staff in the period following the death of his father has meant Hani is now doing well in school and excelling in science, a field his father taught in the local UNRWA school. It is clear that Hani is filling the position of man of the house as he sits quietly with his mother and watches over his younger brothers. Ahmed, the youngest, was four months when Arafa died, "he did not have a chance to know or to love his father" says Imtihan.

Speaking of the future Imtihan is hopeful, "I have four young boys whom I hope to see graduate from college and get married, but I am only one, it is a huge responsibility and I must be strong." She is also hopeful for prospects regarding legal proceedings in Israel concerning compensation for her husband's killing given that Arafa was clearly not a military target at the time of his killing at the hands of Israeli occupation forces.

DAY 10
MON 5ᵀᴴ JANUARY

In Dublin it is bitterly cold still. There is more fighting in Gaza. A Irish political journalist suggested Jaber Wishah could be interviewed on Morning Ireland but John Ging had already been lined up. He is also an excellent choice to talk on the humanitarian crisis. Sadly, once again, his information is 'balanced' by the Israeli ambassador who comes out with the same party line. Do all Israeli spokespeople go to the same assertive training school? They all sound similar and repeat the same statements over and over again regardless of the question.

There are some casualties among Israeli soldiers and news that eighty men who are accused of being Hamas have been picked up. Clare says no one knows where they have been taken. This is horrifying because from my experience with former prisoners most of them are badly tortured and many remain without charge for years in prison. Some of these men may be guilty of crimes but without a trial we will never know the truth. My heart sinks at the thought of this. Clare is contacting the Red Cross on behalf of her human rights organisation Addameer. (In October 2022 six human rights organisations were accused of being terrorist organizations, Addameer was one of them. Its office in Ramallah was raided and all the computers and files were confiscated. One French Palestinian lawyer Falah Hammouri was arbitrarily detained and jailed under administrative detention for a year.)

AMAL AL-SAMOUNI

(Official testimony from Palestinian Centre of Human Rights)

"I have constant pain in my head, eyes and ears. I have been having nose bleeds for the past three years. I can still feel the shrapnel move inside my brain"

5th January 2009

On 4 January 2009 at around 6:00 Israeli forces surrounded the house where Amal al-Samouni (11) and 18 members of her extended family were sheltering, in Zeitoun neighborhood east of Gaza City. Israeli soldiers ordered the owner of the house, Amal's father Attia al-Samouni (37), to step outside with his hands up. Upon opening the door he was immediately killed by shots to the head and chest. Soldiers then started firing bullets into the house, killing Amal's 4-year old brother Ahmad al-Samouni and injuring at least 4 other people, of whom 2 were children.

Over the following hours, soldiers ordered over 100 other members of the extended al-Samouni family into the house of Wa'el Fares Hamdi al-Samouni, Amal's uncle. On 5 January 2009 Israeli forces directly targeted the house and its vicinity, killing 21 persons and injuring many others. Amal, who was inside, was wounded by shrapnel to the head and buried under the rubble, lying between injured, dying and deceased relatives. On 7 January ambulance personnel, who were prevented from entering the area until then, evacuated her to hospital.

Between 4-7 January 2009, 27 members of the Samouni family were killed, including 11 children and 6 women, and 35 others were injured, including Amal's twin brother Abdallah.

Amal survived those 4 horrific days but is left with permanent injuries and trauma. "I remember my brother and father and how they were murdered in every moment," says Amal as she thinks back on the attacks and the three days she spent buried under the rubble of her uncle's house without food or water. Amal does not need a lot of words to express how she feels: "before, we used to live together as a happy family. Now I don't feel happy anymore."

Amal did not only lose her father; the family's home was also destroyed by the army. "For one year we lived with the parents of my mother, in Gaza's Shaja'iya neighborhood. Then we lived in a storage room for 1.5 years. It didn't have a floor. There was just sand. Since 6 months we are living where our old house used to be. It is not even half the size of our old home. I didn't want to return to our neighborhood because of what happened. My family didn't want to either but we had no choice." Like many other members of the al-Samouni family,

Amal's household now receives some help from relatives living in their neighborhood, but is still struggling to manage financially. The living conditions of Amal and her family have somewhat improved over time, although the house still lacks equipment like a refrigerator, washing machine, and a closet for the children's clothing. Amal's father, Attia, was a farmer. He grew vegetable crops on a rented plot, which used to provide the family income.

As the reconstruction of life and livelihoods continues in the al-Samouni neighborhood, Amal continues to struggle with her injuries. The pieces of shrapnel embedded in her brain cause her severe pains. Local doctors say it would be too dangerous to remove the pieces, but Amal cannot accept this quite yet. She has a strong wish to travel abroad to see a doctor. "I want to be sure about my situation and have another doctor look at my situation. I want to try everything possible to end my problem and pain. Other children are sometimes able to travel for fun. My wish is serious; I won't travel for amusement but for medical treatment."

The continuous pain has a profound impact on Amal's mood, her relationship with her siblings, and her performance in school. "When I have a lot of pain I become nervous and angry." Her mother Zeinat (38) adds that "she then easily becomes angry with her younger siblings and beats them. Recently she and I visited a hospital again to see how she could be helped. The doctor prescribed tramal [a sedative] but I will not allow her to take medicine like that."

"When I am sad I go to my aunt's house to see my cousins, or I prepare my books for school," says Amal. "Before the war I was excellent in school. Now my scores are not so good anymore." While speaking of her dropped scores Amal becomes very emotional. The teacher told her mother that Amal is not able to focus in class. This semester Amal failed two subjects. "I have pain in my eyes when I look at the blackboard," Amal says, very upset. Despite her difficulties in school, Amal knows what she would like to study for: "when I am older I want to become a pediatrician and help to treat wounded people."

PCHR submitted a criminal complaint to the Israeli authorities on behalf of the al-Samouni family on 8 May 2009. To-date, only an interlocutory response has been received, noting receipt of the complaint. Despite repeated requests, no further information has been received.

DAY 11
TUES 6ᵀᴴ JANUARY

The coldest night so far, the thick layer of frost glistening on the trees is quite beautiful. Obama says he is concerned about civilian casualties but he still can't say anything about the conflict until he enters office as there is only one president. As one journalist points out, does that mean that he's happy to go along with the words of Bush? I ring some friends in the US, one of them, Professor Alice Bach says this is giving the green light to Israel letting them know that they have two weeks in which to bomb as much as they want. This is what happened in Lebanon two years ago. The inability of the West to criticize the actions of Israel, led them to believe that they could do anything. As they are one of the biggest military machines in the world, I suppose that makes sense. (In 2023\4 even more atrocities were carried out as we can see from the horrific number of dead.)

Alice also says that there are a thousand people demonstrating in Cleveland which apparently is a large number in that part of America.

Cover up

Two UNRWA schools are bombed. Israeli government spokesman Mark Regev justifies the bombing by saying that militants were sheltering there along with civilians. To attempt to prove it they have two names of Hamas militants whom they say are involved. I don't understand this point; it doesn't seem to prove anything. The UN says they will investigate. During my time training staff with the UNRWA in Gaza and the West Bank, I have seen no evidence whatsoever of the UN allowing any militant activities. I have the greatest respect for UNRWA which has a very tough task feeding and caring for thousands of refugees and is greatly hampered in its work by Israel. (Israel has always targeted UNRWA over the years and the only reason I can give for this is that UNRWA is responsible for the welfare of the Palestinians.) A few years ago a group of American congressmen and women complained to UNRWA that even their textbooks were encouraging violence. Of course, no occupying power likes the factual information about their occupation to be exposed. My first job after I qualified in the UK was at Queen's University Belfast in the early 1970s. During that time a lot of British military activities in Ireland were covered up, including the infamous "Bloody Sunday" in 1972.

Gordon Brown says this is the Middle East's darkest hour and all must work on the humanitarian crisis – what about the crisis of justice?

AL-DAYAH FAMILY

(Official testimony from Palestinian Centre of Human Rights)

"The bodies of nine of those killed were not found, including the bodies of my wife and my children. I tried my best with the civil defense personnel to find their bodies. All we found were pieces of flesh that were unidentifiable."

6th January 2009

On 6 January 2009, at approximately 05:45, an Israeli aircraft bombed the al-Dayah family in the Zeitoun neighborhood of Gaza City. 22 people, including 12 children and a pregnant woman, were killed. Only one of the family members inside the house at the time of the attack, Amer al-Dayah (31), survived. Amer, two brothers who had not yet returned home from Morning Prayer at a nearby mosque, and two sisters who live elsewhere with their husbands and children are the only surviving members of the al-Dayah family.

Mohammed al-Dayah (31) recalls the day of the attack: "after I finished praying, I stood beside the mosque, talking to our neighbor, waiting for the sound of the airplanes and bombardments in the area to decrease. Then I heard a very powerful explosion. Shrapnel landed where I was standing. I immediately rushed home. When I reached it, I only found a pile of rubble. I began screaming and calling out for members of my family, but there was no reply. They were all under the rubble. Dead."

"At the moment I cannot imagine ever being happy again, or celebrating a happy occasion. It reminds me of the old life I used to have with my family. Before, I used to go to many parties. I always danced dabke, together with my extended family in Zeitoun. I led the dancing. Whenever we had a chance to celebrate, we would. Now I cannot bear the sound of party music, of celebrations. It makes me too sad. Whenever there is a party in the neighborhood, I have to leave the house and go somewhere else," says Mohammed. The holidays are the most difficult time of the year for him: "during Ramadan and the Eid holidays I suffer and think of them even more than usual."

His brother 'Amer pushed Mohammed to remarry. "At first I didn't want to but I was alone and I had to somehow rebuild a life," says Mohammed. Now Mohammed is remarried and has two daughters, Amani (4 months) and Qamar (1.5 years old), both named after his daughters who died in the attack. "I didn't make a party when I remarried. Neither did my brothers for their weddings. We simply do not feel like celebrating anything."

Mohammed works as an electrician with the Ministry of Health, but has had difficulties at his work since he lost his family. "I am not able to sleep at night. The night time is the most difficult part of the day for me as I cannot fall asleep. I have tried everything. Even medicine, but that only made me dizzy. So, at night I just stay up and keep myself busy; eating, taking a walk, sitting in the cemetery, going for a run. Only after sunrise I fall asleep for a few hours, exhausted. Then, how can I go to work in time? I can't. My boss has given me 10 warnings so far but at the same time I know that he understands and has sympathy for my situation."

The three brothers rebuilt a house on the same place as the old building. All three of them insisted to return to the same location. "It is where we grew up," says Mohammed. "The Ministry of Works assisted us in constructing the base and first floor of the house, but the bomb left a seven meter deep hole under the building which affected the foundation and ground water. It took us 3 months to fix the water problem, before we could even start construction of a new building." However, Mohammed still notices that there are problems with the foundation of the building. "Every time there is a bombing, I feel the house move. It wasn't like that before. The house is not steady. The base was destroyed by the bomb."

As Mohammed tries to rebuild a life and a future, he has no hopes that he will see those responsible for the death of his family being held accountable. "I expect nothing from Israeli Courts. They [Israel] prepare a plan and justification first and then carry out their attack. The war crimes are justified before being committed. Crimes could happen anytime again."

PCHR submitted a criminal complaint to the Israeli authorities on behalf of the al-Dayah family on 18 May 2009. To-date, no response has been received.

DAY 12
WED 7ᵀᴴ JANUARY

Clare says many have been killed again today. She is very tired and working long hours. The campaign for administrative detention that she has been working on for the last 6 months had to be shelved because of the Gaza crisis. Shimon Peres is interviewed on the news. The interviewer starts in quite a tough fashion about the UNRWA schools but Peres answers like a kindly grandfather and the interviewer softens. By some people, Peres is seen as a man of peace who has received the Nobel peace prize; but many Israelis view him as a hardline Zionist.

Finally there is a truce of three hours to get supplies into Gaza. The first truce finished six minutes early, the TV reporter hearing artillery fire says it must be the Israelis. In the next report he changed it to gunfire and was much more vague and ambiguous. This was then followed by a report about Qassam rockets - no ambiguity there. I am afraid. Israel describes Egyptian-French peace deal as a work in progress. That allows them some time for more bombing.

The first sign of hope is when Israel says it has accepted, in principal, the Egyptian-French plan. The Independent newspaper reports that the tunnels are being used to bring food into Gaza. I don't think there is any mention of the smuggling of weapons.

The Israeli cabinet opted to continue the offensive. Yesterday there was an estimated twenty nine deaths and there are reports that Turkish forces are being considered for the Rafah-Egyptian border.

I spend some time working on my lectures for college. This term I am lecturing on the psychology of personality theory. As I work on the writing of the great theorists - Freud, Jung, Frankl, Maslow and Rogers - I wonder what they would have thought of this situation.

THE MATTAR FAMILY

(Official testimony from Palestinian Centre of Human Rights)

"It would be great if someone could take me to the dessert and leave me there, that way I wouldn't have to see people"

7th January 2009

At around 09:30 on 7 January 2009, Israeli forces targeted the al-Taqwa Mosque in the Sheikh Radwan district of Gaza City. The mosque was 150 metres from the home of Mahmoud Mattar, who was 14 at the time. Having run to the scene of the attack, Mahmoud was present when two further strikes hit the area, killing two 15 year old boys, including one of Mahmoud's school friends. Mahmoud was thrown unconscious and suffered severe burns and shrapnel wounds. He has been left totally blind as a result.

Mahmoud tells of the changes in his life since the attack: "I used to go by myself to the sea. I was independent. Now I need someone to go with me everywhere I go. I go out maybe once every two or three months, I spend my days inside." Mahmoud's self awareness of his injuries means he is now afraid to go out and be amongst people. "I don't want to go out due to the comments I get from children. Anytime I do I cover my face with my clothes and dark glasses", says Mahmoud. "The glasses broke yesterday."

The emotional and physical scars of 7 January 2009 have taken their toll on Mahmoud. Keeping his head lowered into his chest and pausing to catch his breath as a result of breathing problems related to transplanted bone matter in his nose, Mahmoud says he is not the young man who spoke with such optimism for the future, in spite of his injuries, three years ago. "When I was in Egypt for medical treatment and when I got back to Gaza everything was calm and people were so supportive of me. But things changed, people started fighting and it's always noisy. The change you see is out of my hands."

Mahmoud has been left anxious and short tempered. "I have become very nervous since the attack. If someone is kidding with me I will try to hit them with anything at hand," says Mahmoud. His anger has resulted in problems in school, for which he was suspended for a year. "As a result of my rushed reaction to incidents there are problems between me and the teachers as well as other students."

Mahmoud has also had to adapt to the new challenges he faces, including learning brail, which took him a year of dedicated study. Mahmoud was in Grade 9 at the time of the attack three years ago, he is now in Grade 10.

Mahmoud's anxiety complicates his family life with his parents and siblings as well as his school life. "Mahmoud is a good guy," says his father Hani, "but he can be problematic, including being violent with me. But I understand, I am patient with him." His mother Randa, 38 adds; "he can be very destructive, including taking his anger out physically on the home or his little brother."

Speaking of the future, Mahmoud says: "before the attack I played lots of sport and I had wanted to be a PE teacher or to open a sports club. But all these hopes are destroyed. Now my only wish is to leave my formal education and focus on my religion and learn the Koran".

Mahmoud hopes to eventually receive surgery to clear his breathing, as well as reconstructive plastic surgery, which he says has been promised to him by many charity organisations, all of whom have failed to deliver; "If I could get the surgery I would be more comfortable amongst people."

Like any young man, he also has dreams to be married, but his parents say there is no room in the house for another young family.

Mahmoud is dismissive regarding the prospect of justice before Israeli courts. "I don't expect the case to be successful. The Israeli's are liars; they attack children and are careless in what they target."

PCHR submitted a criminal complaint to the Israeli authorities on behalf of Mahmoud Mattar on 30 December 2009. To-date, no response has been received.

DAY 13
THURSDAY 8ᵀᴴ JANUARY

The news said rockets are being fired from Lebanon. Immediately the worry is that Hezbollah is taking advantage of the situation. Later this information is changed to implicate a Palestinian dissident group rather than Hezbollah. The TV is full of pictures of Israelis running for cover – no point of people in Gaza running for cover – there is no cover. I hope that these images don't add to the already strong Israeli idea of victimhood. Clare is having nightmares about dead bodies after seeing all the TV pictures and is having dreams of Israeli soldiers coming into her house and making arrests. She talks again of soldiers entering houses in Gaza and taking out all the young men and removing them to secret places in Israel. Allegations of many being shot have been made. Clare informed the Red Cross but they are not making the protest that Addameer wanted.

Intimidated

This happened in the 1930s in Germany, all protests went unheard by the world and people were intimidated into silence and the Holocaust was allowed to happen. If the UN and the Red Cross want to carry on their very necessary work, to some extent they have to be careful or they will not be allowed to

A Gaza Diary

stay in the country, let alone adequately carry out their duties. If diplomats tell the story that most governments don't want to hear they will be ignored or recalled. Some of the clergy in Bethlehem and Jerusalem are not able to speak out because otherwise their visas will not be reissued. This all leads to a culture of silence which is the only way to maintain an evil status quo.

"War – every war – is the realm of lies. Whether called propaganda or psychological warfare, everybody accepts that it is right to lie for one's country. Anyone who speaks the truth runs the risk of being branded a traitor."

Uri Avnery – January 2009 -

The politician, Chris Andrews TD, has suggested that Israel should be blamed and not Hamas, he is disregarded because his views are shared by Sinn Fein. Some prominent Israelis, however, also agree with this view.

Johann Hari suggests that; "The sound of Gaza burning should be drowned out by the words of the Israeli writer Larry Derfner. He says "Israel's war with Gaza has to be the most one-sided on earth... If the point is to end it, or at least begin to end it, the ball is not in Hamas's court – it is in ours."

Today a UN truck driver was killed driving supplies during the truce, he was a Palestinian and there would have been more uproar had he been a foreigner. There is further news about the terrible bombing of UNRWA schools which according to the Israelis were harbouring terrorists and weapons. The UN were

A Gaza Diary

privately informed by the Israelis that there were no weapons in the UNRWA schools. Why were they only informed privately? Why not tell the world the truth.

Embarrassed

Several years ago the Israeli army reported that UNRWA was loading weapons onto ambulances. For weeks this news and aerial pictures of the ambulance were flashed around the world on television and in the press. Finally it was admitted that this report was incorrect. This information, unlike the first report, was accompanied by very little media coverage. A top UNRWA official in Gaza, however, told me that he had been telephoned the following morning after the reported accusation by a senior member of the Israeli Defence Forces (IDF) who apologised and said that he was embarrassed because they knew there no weapons in the ambulance. The important images, however, had gone around the world carrying the message that UNRWA was involved in terrorism. I never saw this message openly countered in the press and the admission remained relatively unknown. So the speed of this latest admission about the schools was interesting as was the fact that it was picked up by the press. Maybe things are changing for the better although very slowly.

(Well actually when events of 2023/4 are examined it is obvious that the situation has got much, much worse. There have been so many false accusations of which one of the worst was the destruction of al Shifa Hospital, when the world was told that Hamas had tunnels under the hospital. We were then shown a video of a couple of guns and jackets. Quite laughable if it was not so utterly tragic. An Israeli official admitted that they had 'overestimated' the role played by al Shifa Hospital.

That admission does not help the patients who are going to die because the hospital has been destroyed.)

Suspicious

The Israelis have for a very long time been suspicious of the motives of the UN and other international aid agencies who give humanitarian help to Palestinians. The director of an international aid group was routinely told to undress and strip naked whenever he travelled through Ben Gurion airport and he was then approached by individuals who would slowly put on rubber gloves as an intimidation process. This is a message to international groups dealing with aid to the refugees of Palestine – play the game or stay away.

John Ging is very angry and is excellent in his response to the story about the UN school bombing. A US congressman wrote to Condoleeza Rice to say the Israelis were bombing UNRWA schools with American weapons, a lone voice for peace and justice.

Leaflets

There is news of leaflets being dropped in Gaza telling the people to move as the Israelis would bomb Rafah. Poor Yousef, there is nowhere for him to go, this is horrific news.

Clare tells me there are threats again to bomb al Shifa hospital in Gaza City because the Israelis claim Hamas militants are being treated in the hospital. Twelve more bodies found under the rubble of the UNRWA school, how many bodies are still under the rubble? It reminds me of Lebanon two years ago.

THE AL-RAHEL FAMILY

(Official testimony from Palestinian Centre of Human Rights)

"The other children keep talking about Dima and the memories of both incidents. 'We wish to die like Dima' is what the children sometimes say to me because of all the stress and our poor living conditions."

8th January 2009

On 8 January 2009, at approximately 11:00, four missiles were fired at the house of Juma'a al-Rahel (45) in Beit Lahiya, injuring 3 members of the extended al-Rahel family: Basma (3), Dima (5), and Faten (41). Many of the extended family were inside the house at the time of the attack, as six of the al-Rahel brothers and their wives and children live nearby. Immediately after the attack, the families fled the area and sought refuge in Beit Lahiya's UNRWA school. On 17 January 2009 the school was targeted with white phosphorus bombs, leaving Dima's sister, Ansam al-Rahel (13), severely injured. After six weeks of fighting for her life 5-year old Dima eventually died of her wounds in an Egyptian hospital on 1 March 2009.

Saeed al-Rahel (35), the father of Dima and Ansam, remembers the day of the first attack vividly. "I was at home when an explosion took place and all the windows were broken. I got out of the house. I heard people screaming in the house of my brother Juma'a, nextdoor. My daughter Dima was there and I heard people screaming that she was wounded. Several more missiles struck Juma'a's house and we fled from the area. Dima was taken to hospital. On 13 January she was transferred to Egypt. I went with her."

Saeed's wife, Nisreen al-Rahel (33), and their other children, Sunia (17), Dina (15), Ansam (13), Ahmad (11), Mohammed (6), and Ali (4), stayed in the UNRWA school in Beit Lahiya after the attack. Nisreen recalls: "we stayed in the school building from 8 to 17 January. It was winter and very cold. We didn't have any mattresses. We had to use blankets as mattresses and it was very difficult, especially for the children. We didn't have enough food. We also had to ask other people to give us water. There was no clean water."

On 17 January 2009 the Israeli army bombed the school building with white phosphorus shells. "Experiencing the attack on the school was more difficult for me than the attack on the house. At the moment that the bombing of the school started I was in a classroom with my children. The bombing started around 5:00am and it was dark. I heard Ansam cry 'I am wounded in my head'. The firing of bombs was very intensive." Ansam was severely injured in the head, she lost her hair in the place of the injury and the scars get infected

A Gaza Diary

from time to time as parts of her skull are missing. "She is still suffering because of her injuries. At school she loses consciousness when she is active," say Nisreen.

Saeed remembers the moment he found out about the bombing of the school: "Before I went to Egypt I stayed in that same classroom with my family. I saw the attack on the television when I was in Egypt and I recognized the classroom. There was blood on the floor. When I called to my family, no one wanted to tell me how my daughter Ansam was doing."

When Nisreen and her remaining children moved back to their house after the offensive they found it badly damaged and their livelihood destroyed. "Shortly before the war I bought cattle. We had 2 oxen, 17 goats and dozens of rabbits. I kept them next to our house. I took out loans to buy them," explains Saeed. "When our family returned to our house after the war they found all the animals killed by shrapnel. Only one goat was still alive but he also died after a few days. Now I am stuck with many loans. I can barely provide for the treatment of my daughter Ansam. I was even arrested by the police because I cannot pay back my loans to people. With a complete lack of money I am also not able to repair the severe damage that was done to the windows and walls of our house." Cardboard and blankets serve to protect the family from the nightly and winter cold.

Saeed noticed changes in his children too. "Ansam holds a lot of anxiety and stress since the war. One time I called her and she started screaming and threw a plate at me, screaming to leave her alone. I am her father and she is afraid of me." Nisreen adds: "Ahmad's scores were badly affected after the war. He used to be an excellent student. Now he even has problems in reading. He also suffers from bedwetting."

A Gaza Diary

Fear seems to have become a part of daily life for the family. "The children, like me, are always afraid when they hear drones or firing. When we hear it, we all sit in a single room," says Nisreen. The fear of another attack is never far from Saeed's thoughts either: "I am afraid that another war will come. When people talk about it I feel afraid. When I hear drones in the area, I leave the house. I get afraid that they will target us again."

PCHR submitted a criminal complaint to the Israeli authorities on behalf of the al-Rahel family on 9 September 2009. To-date, no response has been received.

DAY 14
FRI 9ᵀᴴ JANUARY

Amnesty International held a candlelit vigil on Friday evening. We met friends from Amnesty and talked to Labour TD, Proinsias De Rossa, who said he had met Clare when he went with a delegation to Palestine last November. He said he would continue to speak out against the special relationship with the Israelis. Rang Clare, she was just going to the doctor but she told me that another new building has been bombed and eight or nine family members died. Clare is devastated, as are we all, but I hope that in her case, all the stress of Gaza is not affecting her own pregnancy. I am finding that listening to the news is unbearable but because of Clare's role in human rights she has to keep going, unbearable or not.

THE ABU ODA FAMILY

(Official testimony from Palestinian Centre of Human Rights)

"The Israeli military say they are the most moral army in the world, but they killed my daughter, they didn't respect her right to live"

9th January 2009

On 9 January 2009, the Abu Oda household in the Al Amal neighbourhood of Beit Hanoun came under sustained fire from Israeli positions close to the Gaza-Israeli border 2 kilometres away. Nariman Abu Oda, 16, was hit in the right side of her body by Israeli fire as she was walking from the hallway, where the family were taking cover, to the kitchen. Medics were unable to reach the family and Nariman died before she could receive medical attention.

A Gaza Diary

The pockmarked concrete walls of the Abu Oda household tell a good deal of the story of Nariman's death. Despite the best efforts of father Ahmed Abdel Kareem Muhammad, 57, and mother, I'tidal Abd al Aziz, 53, to plaster over the patch work of holes and indentations in the walls, ceiling, floors and doors, the house remains riddled with bullet holes. As I'tidal explains "it is clear the shooting was completely indiscriminate."

The Abu Oda family find themselves caught in a deep state of mourning regarding Nariman's absence, yet at the same time feel her constant presence. Recalling that Nariman used to make him his coffee in the morning, Ahmed says that, he still absentmindedly calls for Nariman when he wants coffee or tea. "Her room is still exactly as she left it three years ago, with everything still in its place." Despite this, the family are desperately seeking to move; "we do not want to live in the house that Nariman was killed in," says Ahmed. Adding to the sense of presence Nariman has in the house, I'tidal and Ahmed's children Shadi, 34, Abdel Kareem, 32, and Sahar, 30, have all since had daughters whom they named Nariman, in the memory of their younger sister.

I'tidal was deeply affected physically and mentally by the loss of her daughter who used to help her a lot with daily household chores. "When I see young girls going to school I imagine her with them, I see her in every room of the house, I will never forget her. After the incident I was admitted to the hospital for ten days due to shock" recalls I'tidal, "since then I have suffered from huge physical problems resulting from stress." I'tidal has health complications relating to blood pressure, heart disease and diabetes.

A Gaza Diary

The family did not only lose Nariman during the Israeli offensive, but also their livelihood. The family had a citrus grove and a poultry farm that were totally destroyed during the attack and have another farm that they cannot reach due to its proximity to the Israeli imposed buffer zone. The family have recently planted seedlings in one of the destroyed farms again but are still waiting to harvest them. However, the loss of income from the farms is mentioned merely as an afterthought to the loss of Nariman. "We care nothing for the loss of our land compared to the loss of our daughter" says Ahmed.

Speaking of the future the couple are desperately seeking answers and demand accountability. "I don't expect the case to be successful, they will change the facts, the only thing I want is to address the soldier who killed my daughter" says Ahmed. "But I hope one day that we can reach peace with the Israeli's and end the war and the killing."

PCHR submitted a criminal complaint to the Israeli authorities on behalf of the Abu Oda Family on 30 August 2009. To-date, no response has been received.

DAY 15
SAT 10ᵀᴴ JANUARY

The T.V. reported that Israel's bombardment continues despite the three hour truce to allow much needed humanitarian aid to be delivered. Yesterday UNRWA was unable to deliver aid because Israel was bombing the trucks. (How tragic! This is the same story fifteen years later. People are starving, aid is not getting into Gaza and still world governments are doing nothing.) Israel drops leaflets to tell Gazan residents it plans 'to escalate' operations. I try to clear to clear my head by walking our dog Kofi in the local park. Kofi was found wandering in the park after we returned from Niall's posting in the UN in New York. Kofi Annan was the UN Secretary-General at the time. Hence the name.

Feeling a bit better I call into my neighbour's house next door. Evelyn has been a great friend for years and always helped me with the registered charity Seamus Cashman and I set up from the sale of my books on Palestine. She is very upset about the situation but - as there is very little on the western news channels - she does not know the real story.

WAFA AL-RADEA

(Official testimony from Palestinian Centre of Human Rights)

"When I left my children I was walking and my children had not seen my wounds. The most difficult moment was when I came back with only 1 leg and many injuries. I was a different Wafa. When I came back I was supposed to happy and the people were supposed to be happy for seeing me but everyone was crying."

10th January 2009

On 10 January 2009, at around 16:30, Wafa al-Radea (39) and her sister Ghada (32) were targeted by two Israeli drone missiles while walking on Haboub street, one of the main roads in Beit Lahiya. The sisters were walking during the Israeli announced hour long ceasefire, and were on their way to a clinic nearby because Wafa felt that she was close to delivering a baby. Both women were severely injured in the attack.

"When people came to help I could hear them speak but was unable to respond. They were saying that I was dead," remembers Wafa. While Ghada was taken to hospital with severe injuries to her legs, people had covered Wafa as they thought she was dead. Eventually an ambulance brought her to a hospital where doctors carried out a caesarean section surgery in an attempt to save her baby. It was only during the surgery the doctors realized Wafa was still alive. While her son, Iyad, was born, doctors amputated Wafa's right leg and attempted to treat her other injuries. On 12 January both sisters were transferred to a hospital in Egypt for additional medical treatment. Wafa underwent a series of operations until the end of April and then had 3 months of rehabilitation. Wafa and Ghada returned to Gaza on 29 and 27 June 2009.

Wafa vividly remembers the months she spent in Egypt. "My clearest memory of that time is the unbearable pain caused by the changing of the bandages. It took nurses 5 to 6 hours each time. I underwent many surgeries. After an operation to transplant skin from my left thigh to a lower part of my leg, nurses removed the transplanted cells by mistake when cleaning the wound. I had to undergo the same surgery again, this time taking skin from my arms. I was screaming because of the pain. My brother Walid (25) lost consciousness and was bleeding from his nose. He couldn't bear what was happening to me. I was very angry at everyone after the operation." Wafa's brother Walid was with her throughout the whole period in Egypt. She didn't see my other relatives from Gaza. "It was very difficult for them to visit me because travelling to Egypt is costly and they had to look after the children," she says.

A Gaza Diary

Wafa is the mother of 8 children: Ehab (20), Lina (19), Hani (17), Shourouq (15), Mo'taz (13), Saher (12), Jehad (9), and Iyad (3). During her time in Egypt Wafa had limited contact with her children. She says: "in the first 3 months I couldn't speak to my children over the phone. I refused. I was unable to talk. They were waiting for me for 6 months. The children were curious to know what happened to me."

Wafa's eldest daughters, Lina (19) and Shourouq (16) had taken care of Iyad while their mother was in hospital in Egypt. "One of them would go to school in the morning and leave Iyad with her sister. In the afternoon it was the other way around." She continues: "when I came home they brought Iyad and put him on my lap. He was blond and beautiful and I thought he was a nephew. I couldn't imagine that he was my son. I asked them about Iyad and they told me that he was on my lap." Wafa takes a lot of strength from having her children around her. She says "I am very grateful and happy for having my children. They help me with everything and keep my morale high. Even when I am sad, I would smile if my children came to me. I want them to feel that I am happy because I am with them."

Wafa finds it difficult to accept help from her children: "I always used to be the one who would help them. Before, I used to go to the school to check on the children and walk to the market to do the shopping. Now if want to go out I must use a car. And if I want to move in the house I must use a wheelchair. I also use the walkers and if Iyad wants to take my hand I cannot give him my hand because I am afraid that I will fall. I need my hands to hold the walkers."

Wafa received one year of physiotherapy in Gaza for her back, pelvis and her left leg. Despite several attempts, so far she has no prosthetic leg. She also still undergoes treatment for her left leg. "My leg is getting better but I am still in hospital from time to time, for example when I have inflammations. One month ago I was in hospital for 6 days. In winter my wounds hurt more and I feel pain in my pelvis, back, abdomen and legs."

Despite constantly being confronted with the past Wafa tries to focus on the future. "I hope that our children will not have to pass through similar experiences when they are older. I wish that their lives will be better. But my children keep asking me 'will there be another war, come again and kill us all?' They are afraid and I see how the war negatively impacted on them," she says.

Wafa feels great frustration over how the crime against her and her sister caused so much suffering and yet goes unpunished. "It has been 3 years since they [Israel] attacked us and there is still no response. I spoke to many people from human rights organizations about my story and what is the result of it? There is no result or action whatsoever."

PCHR submitted a criminal complaint to the Israeli authorities on behalf of Wafa al-Radea on 07 October 2009. To-date, no response has been received.

DAY 16
SUN 11ᵀᴴ JANUARY

Official numbers, eight hundred and seventy-four Palestinians are dead. Thirteen Israelis of whom ten are soldiers, many killed by friendly fire. Olmert claims Israel is close to achieving goals in the Gaza Strip and there will be no let up. (Sounds like Netanyahu in the latest conflict.)

There are reports of an incident of shelling without warning in Beit Lahya. Four women were killed by tank fire. Today twenty-nine Palestinians have been killed and over half of these are reported to be civilians.

There are reports of the Israeli War Cabinet being divided and in a state of disagreement. What a chilling phrase – 'War Cabinet.' A major military power against the starving population of Gaza. This has shades of another conflict in Poland and Germany in the last century. In this "War Cabinet" some apparently accepted limited goals, others want to bring about the collapse of Hamas.

The Hamas leader in Syria is sending out mixed messages – at first accepting a ceasefire and then talking of fighting to the death. They are reporting in Syria that the Israeli action is bringing about resistance in every household. Is this not causing more terrorism and more hatred ask some people in bewilderment and if so, why behave this way? (Military action is rarely the answer as we can see in Gaza in 2024. Now we are possibly in danger of a major war as the US and the UK target the Houtis in Yemen, the Israelis target the Hesbollah in Lebanon and the US is targeting Iranian-backed groups in Syria and Iraq.)

At night we go out for for a quiet dinner with friends Eric and Hilda as it's my birthday. Both of them have stayed with us in Palestine and are very worried about the events in Gaza.

Wrong Premise

Although most people in Israel are behind the military action in Gaza and believe the pictures are staged, many others, both in Israel and in the rest of the world, feel that the actions are leading to more long-term problems and terrorism. Maybe the reason we can't understand this behaviour is because we are starting from the wrong premise. We all assume that the Israeli government wants peace. Sadly, some Israelis acknowledge that not only does the government not want peace but cannot allow it. The plan, according to excellent Israeli academic Ilan Pappé, is ethnic cleansing. There is no longer room for the two-state solution, which is parroted by many Western heads of government, unless there is radical dismantling of settlements and other problems are tackled. A West Bank peppered with illegal settlements and infrastructure near which no Palestinian can live is not a viable and just solution. The Israeli government have not yet bowed to foreign pressure and are continuing to build illegal settlements despite some criticism. Meanwhile Palestinian houses continue to be bulldozed to make way for the illegal building of settlements as new settlers continue to enter Israel and live in the West Bank.

Confirmation

The fact that the UNRWA school was bombed and rockets were not fired from the school by militants is now confirmed. The Israeli spokesman will not acknowledge this fact and continues to state that "we stand by it". He goes on to assert that the firing was from an adjacent building. He also suggested that soldiers did not know it was a UN school. The UN said the Israeli army had the coordinates. At the very least it is gross inefficiency from one of the foremost military powers in the world: if not inefficiency, then it is surely a war crime. Israeli political activist Uri Avnery accused the army spokesman of telling lies, saying that no Hamas militants were in the school, just terrified refugees.

Deputy Israeli Prime Minister Ramon thinks Israel should go further in its hostilities.

One of the Pope's representatives, Cardinal Martini, whom we knew when we lived in Jerusalem for many years and who knows the situation very well, compared Israeli actions in Gaza to the Holocaust. At least that should start some discussion.

The U.N. schools are now acting as shelter for twenty-five thousand Palestinians.

THE HAMOUDA FAMILY

(Official testimony from Palestinian Centre of Human Rights)

"I cannot even pick up another child in my arms, I had a new grandchild, he is six months old, but I have yet to take him in my arms, I feel that place belongs to Fares"

11th January 2009

In the early morning of 11 January 2009, the home of Intissar Hamouda, 41, in Tal Al-Hawa. Gaza City, came under attack from Israeli forces. Israeli tank fire resulted in the death of her son, Fares Hamouda, who was two years old at the time of the attack, and her step son Muhammed who she cared for with her husband Talat, 54, Muhammed's father. Fares died immediately in Intissar's arms, while Muhammed bled to death as medical crews were unable to reach them.

"Muhammed and Fares had a lot in common. After I had Fares I could not breastfeed so we had to give him manufactured milk. Muhammed lost his mother at ten months and so was also fed manufactured baby milk. As a result, both had similar illnesses with similar symptoms," says Intissar. Throughout their brief time together the brothers remained close. "Fares would refuse to go to sleep until Muhammed came home from school. On the day of the attack Fares was sick, but he refused to take medicine from me, he wanted it from Muhammed," says Intissar.

Following the attack Intissar was severely debilitated. "I could not walk on my legs even six months after the incident due to injuries in my legs and pelvis; I needed help from my step daughters and sisters to move around the house." Intissar has since undergone three surgeries to remove shrapnel from her abdomen as well as reconstructive plastic surgery.

Fares was not only close to his half brother Muhammed, but also to Intissar's step daughter Kariman and step grandchild Rania, who were 13 and 2 respectively at the time of the incident. Both have been traumatised as a result. "Kariman became extremely aggressive in school and at the advice of teachers Talat decided to withdraw her from it," says Imtissar. "Three months following the incident I came back to the house with Rania to get her toys and other things, but she begged me not to enter the house and wouldn't take anything from it." Similarly, Intissar said that "ten days ago we were in the Old City shopping and Rania saw a funeral of someone killed in a recent Israeli attack, it reminded Rania of Fares and Muhammed and she started to cry, when I explained they had gone to heaven, she replied, "just like Muhammed and Fares"."

A Gaza Diary

As regards the future the couple feel they have nothing left to be taken from them. "We lost the nearest things to us, we have nothing else left to lose," says Intissar. "I am no longer even afraid of the bombings." However Intissar clings to some hope that she can have another child following the death of Fares, who she tried to conceive for 21 years. "I have tried through artificial insemination already, but it didn't work. I'm hoping to try again." Similarly Talat has hopes that there will be political reconciliation among the Palestinian political factions. Regarding the prospects of their complaint in Israeli courts, Intissar is unimpressed; "the Israeli's committed war crimes against us, they destroy the houses over the heads of civilians, I expect no justice from them."

PCHR submitted a criminal complaint to the Israeli authorities on behalf of the Hamouda Family on 21 July 2009. To-date, no response has been received.

DAY 17
MON 12ᵀᴴ JANUARY

Clare rings to tell me that her husband's mother is not well. She has poor health and the stress of news of the slaughter from Gaza cannot be helping her situation. The news on the job front in Ireland continues to deteriorate. Three thousand more jobs are lost. Waterford-Wedgwood is in trouble as are many other businesses.

Bush gives his final news conference. I think, regretfully, of the way the world has gone since his election. Evil is a word that comes to mind since the rise of the neo-cons. The evil of war, the evil of power and the evil of greed. Evil seems rarely to succeed if coming solely from the bottom. The integrity or lack of it at the top of any institution is what seems to make the difference.

Hopefully the Obama regime will be better but I no longer believe that it will make any difference. His silence has shown that.

The Israelis are using prisoners as "human shields" and Clare is in touch with the Red Cross.

THE AYAD FAMILY

(Official testimony from Palestinian Centre of Human Rights)

12th January 2009

On 12 January 2009, the Ayad family home in the Zaytoon area of Gaza City was bulldozed by Israeli forces. Rezeq Ayad, 60, his wife Yusra, 58, and their four sons Mustafa, 16, Muhammed, 20, Abdel Kareem 26, and Khalil, 29, and Khalil's two daughters were left homeless as a result of the attack. The family had left the area a few days prior to the destruction of their home, as a result of the intense Israeli bombardment of the area.

Speaking to Rezeq Ayad and his son, Abdel Kareem, the relief they feel having put their displacement behind them is clear. Now back in the family home – which they started rebuilding in May 2010 and moved into in October 2010 – the two are glad and thankful that the family are now safe and relatively secure once again. "I remember that time and I just thank God we are all still alive," says Rezeq.

"We had left the house with nothing but the clothes we were wearing and a few blankets and mattresses," explains Abdel Kareem, "we lost everything with the house when it was bulldozed." In the aftermath of the attack the whole family were forced to find alternative shelter. "I and my wife moved to relatives in Asqoula in Gaza City," says Rezeq, "my son Abdel Kareem was forced to move to the al Samouni neighbourhood and my son Khalil had no choice but to spend two years in a tent camp with his wife and young daughters."

Rezeq's son, Muhammed Ayad, who was 17 at the time, built a small structure among the ruins of the family home and stayed there so he could watch over the house and his donkeys, which he kept in the area.

Abdel Kareem and his wife Shaheera, 22, spent a little over a year in a makeshift hut that he built from corrugated iron and plastic. "My wife is from the al Samouni family; after the massacre of the al Samouni's in that area during the war she didn't want to move there out of fear of another attack taking place. But we had nowhere else to go." Abdel Kareem describes the conditions the couple endured over that year as "intolerable." "During the summer it was unbearably hot, during the winter, unbearably cold."

Shaheera was pregnant with the young couple's first child at the time the couple were homeless. "There was no running water or electricity in the hut. Shaheera would have to wait for me to come home from work to bring her water. Her pregnancy was very difficult. I was working selling vegetables and transporting goods to save money to build my house," says

A Gaza Diary

Abdul Kareem, "the day we moved in my wife gave birth to my little girl Ru'al." Reflecting on the incident Abdul stresses that he would be unwilling to put himself and his family through the same experience once more. "If there is another war I won't be moving, even if we die there, I don't want to go through that again."

Khalil Ayad, his wife Nabila and their daughters Islam, 5, and Gadeer, 4, were also forced into haphazard makeshift accommodation after the attack. "Khalil went to a tent camp in the Zaytoon area of Gaza. There were a lot of families displaced during the war that moved there temporarily. But Khalil's was the last family to leave. They spent two years there in total" says Rezeq. "They would collect firewood to cook and boil water and they shared a common well with the rest of the camp residents for water." During this experience, Nabila gave birth to, Rezeq, now 1. Like Shaheera, Nabila's pregnancy occurred under very difficult circumstances.

Talking of the future, Abdel Kareem's hopes are simple. "I hope to be strong enough to continue my life and to be a good man" he says. As regards the families complaint with the Israeli government Rezeq and Abdel Kareem are dismissive of any potential for redress; "We don't expect anything from the case. The house was a small home in a quiet residential neighbourhood. It was clearly not a military target. The soldiers knew what they were doing; they just wanted to destroy it. They will not investigate."

Discussing how he was able to rebuild the family home following its destruction Rezeq explains that he had savings from his time as a school teacher in a local UNRWA school. Talking about what he had planned to do with the money he had saved over a lifetime, prior to spending it all on repairing the damage caused by the Israeli military, Rezeq says that he had hoped to help his sons with their marriage and their education. "I spent everything I had saved," says Rezeq with a smile and a shrug of his shoulders, "so now I start again."

PCHR submitted a criminal complaint to the Israeli authorities on behalf of the Ayad family on 2 August 2009. To-date, no response has been received.

DAY 18
TUES 13ᵀᴴ JANUARY

There are accusations of phosphorus bombs being used in Gaza. There were allegations of this during the Lebanese bombings of 2006. I saw pictures on Al-Jazeera of terrible burns and Clare is talking of seeing similar pictures from Gaza.

The IDF spokesperson denies using any bombs that are not used by other countries – which of course is not denying the use of phosphorus bombs. (In the UN Fact Finding Mission of 2009 it was found that Israel did use white phosphorus in densely populated areas.)

Israel is drawing close to the centre of Gaza and is still refusing to let in journalists.

Around the clock Israel's relentless attack goes on in this tiny strip crowded with innocent civilians. A Fatah target is also destroyed.

The news from Gaza city is very upsetting because of the intense bombardment. The hospitals cannot answer ambulance calls. The head of the International Committee of the Red Cross in Gaza says: "There is no place safe in Gaza for the civilians. They're afraid to stay home. They're afraid to move. They're also afraid to go down the street to try to find some water or to try to buy some food. No electricity, no water,

A Gaza Diary

difficult access to hospitals, ambulances that are not able to reach some places to collect the wounded." Pictures are incomplete because of the lack of journalists in Gaza. Still most Israelis believe that right is on their side. As Israelis are not allowed into Gaza they don't know what is going on. I would like to think that if they saw the true picture they would feel otherwise.

HIBBA AL-NAJJAR

(Official testimony from Palestinian Centre of Human Rights)

"The first two years I could manage but this year I have been suffering a lot from the loss of my mother. When I see girls from my school with their mother or talking about their mother, I miss my mother even more. I need to have her with me."

13th January 2009

In the early morning of 13 January 2009, following two days of home demolitions, the Israeli army started to shell the village of Khuza'a and its surroundings, using high explosive and white phosphorous artillery shells. Israeli bulldozers, tanks and snipers were located on the edge of the village. At around 7:00 soldiers ordered the residents of eastern Khuza'a, to leave the area and move towards the centre of the village. Holding a white flag, Rawhiya al-Najjar (47) led a group of approximately 20 women in an attempt to leave as ordered.

Shortly after the group turned the first corner a soldier shot and killed Rawhiya. Another woman in the group, Yasmin al-Najjar (23), was injured by two bullets when she tried to take Rawhiya off the road. Medical staff who tried to evacuate Rawhiya's body were shot at and had to take refuge in a nearby house, and were only able to take the body from the street after more than 10 hours.

"I can still hear the bullet hit my mother in the head. I was standing right beside her when the soldier stepped into the doorway of the house ahead and shot her. I could see him," says Rawhiya's 17 year old daughter Hibba as she depicts the situation with her arms. "I keep wondering why they killed my mother while she was carrying a white cloth in the street, but why I was not killed when I was on the roof of our house earlier that morning." Hibba still cannot make sense of what happened that day.

Hibba is an the only child. She lives with her father, Naser, his second wife, Nuha, and their three children. Her father married Nuha when it became clear that Rawhiya was not able to have any more children and convinced him to marry a second wife. Naser became unemployed after the full closure on the Gaza Strip was imposed. Now the family is dependent on aid and shared agriculture with relatives on lands next to the village, close to the border with Israel.

From the day of the incident Hibba and her family stayed away from the house for two weeks, saying it was too dangerous to move in that part of Khuza'a. For the two months

A Gaza Diary

after that they only went to their house during the daytime and spent the night at the house of relatives in a safer area.

Since the death of her mother Hibba suffers from nightmares, insomnia, stress, and bedwetting. "Before, I would sleep immediately. Now I can't get to sleep at night," says Hibba. Sometimes her father finds her sleepwalking and talking about her mother. Lately she has also begun to experience blurry vision and dizziness. When Hibba started to lose her hair a few months ago, Naser took his daughter to a hospital. The doctor told Hibba and her father that she needs to spend some time outside of the Gaza Strip. Naser is thinking of taking her to Egypt for a little while next summer. However, the closure and high costs make this option far from easy. Hibba says she would like to go out of Gaza but adds that "it will not make me forget anything."

Hibba's schoolwork has also been affected by the traumatic experience and death of her mother. "My mother used to help me with my homework and I used to be very good at school. Now my grades are lower and I am not able to focus in class. When I open a book I feel tired and remember my mother. Even when I study well for an exam, I often forget everything during the exam," she says. Hibba enjoys subjects like Islamic religion and geography but feels sad knowing her scores have dropped a lot. This is the final year of high school for Hibba. However, she doesn't think about what comes after the final exams next summer; "I don't want to think long-term."

Hibba does not like the month of January as it reminds here of the time of the offensive. However, she says 13 January is like any other day for her, "there is no difference with other days because I remember my mother every day regardless." When she feels most sad she usually takes a chair and sits outside the house for a while. Sometimes talking to relatives and her best friend, who is also her neighbour, brings some relief. Hibba is glad to have such a good friend who tries to support her; "I can tell her everything. Without my friend I would have crumbled under the pressure of my loss."

Hibba does not think about the future but rather relives what happened to her and her mother on 13 January 2009. "Since the morning I have been thinking a lot of the incident and how we left my mother in the street," she says, having to pause after every few words. Many things in daily life remind her of her old life with and her future without her mother. "Whenever I see an old woman in the street I wonder if I will still have a clear memory of my mother when I am at that age."

Discussing PCHR's submission of complaints to the Israeli authorities regarding the killing of her mother, Hibba says she does not care: "Nothing can compensate for the loss of my mother but I wish that the soldier who shot my mother will be brought to justice."

PCHR submitted a criminal complaint to the Israeli authorities on behalf of the al-Najjar family on 23 June 2009. To-date, no response has been received.

DAY 19
WED 14ᵀᴴ JANUARY

Cannot believe that the bombing of Gaza is continuing against a background of world silence. In the USA the only news at the moment is about the inauguration of President Obama in a few days time. When Niall and I attended a peace conference in the US in 2008, the Palestinian ambassador to the United Nations told us that Obama had apologised to him for not speaking out on behalf of the Palestinians before the election and said he would speak out when the election was over.

(After his inauguration, Obama again did not speak out nor did he in his second term of office. He was a great disappointment to many people. Former President Jimmy Carter was unique as being the only American leader to take a principled stand on Palestine.)

MUHAMMED MOUSA

(Official testimony from Palestinian Centre of Human Rights)

"We would stay up late at night talking with each other about what had happened over the day, we were brothers, if ever I needed anything I could go to them and they would help me out"

14th January 2009

On 14 January 2009, at approximately 21:00, Israeli aircraft targeted the Mousa family home near al Sabra pharmacy in the south of Gaza City. Izz Addin Wahid Mousa, 48, his wife, Maysara Afif Mousa, 48, their sons Wahid Izz Addi Mousa, 28, Ahmed Izz Addi Mousa, 27, Mohammed Izz Addi Mousa, 22, and daughter Nour Izz Addi Mousa, 15, were killed in the attack.

The physical scars caused by the attack are still clearly visible on 25 year old Muhammad Mousa. With nerve and bone damage in both his right arm and leg he has been left with

A Gaza Diary

a strong limp and his face displays patches of taut skin showing where he was burnt from the fire that engulfed his home. His injuries have left him unable to continue working in the local marble factory, leaving him unable to pick up the pieces of his life after losing his father, mother, sister and three brothers.

Like many who lost their homes during the offensive, Muhammad, has been forced to move frequently. He has moved five times in the intervening period and, with another years rent due on his current home and no way to pay it, has not yet found stability and security. "After the attack I started rebuilding the destroyed home, but I couldn't bear to live there, the incident would keep flooding back into my memory," says Muhammad. "I went to live with my uncle, Hani, but he has a family of his own so I could not stay there."

Emotionally, Muhammad has found himself hugely altered since the war and has had trouble sleeping since the incident. "At first I could not sleep at night at all, I would sit awake all night and might sleep for a while in the morning." He now needs help doing basic things that others take for granted, such as preparing food to eat, which leaves him short tempered. "I lose patience very quickly, when I can't do something myself I get hugely frustrated and become angry." This is compounded by the sense of helplessness he feels regarding medical treatment for his injuries, which he says he was told by doctors is only available in Germany. He still requires extensive medical treatment on bone and nerves in his leg and for shrapnel wounds in his abdomen.

"I was in hospital for four months in Egypt (of which two and half months was in intensive care) without knowing the fate of my family. My sisters had initially told me that they were fine for the sake of my recovery. When I told them I was ready to come home they were forced to tell me the news that they had died, I immediately regressed and had to spend another two weeks in intensive care before being able to go."

Muhammad has fond memories of his deceased brothers Wahid, Ahmed and Mohammad who he was very close to. It is clear he desperately misses their company. "We would stay up late at night talking with each other about what had happened over the day. We were brothers, if ever I needed anything I could go to them and they would help me out." He says they are never far from his mind day or night, asleep or awake.

Muhammad shares the dreams of any young man for his future; he wants to get married, build a home, and one day have children. But he is sceptical his hopes will come true. "How can I provide for a wife and children, I cannot work, I cannot earn a living." While he is optimistic about the outcome of legal action being taken on his behalf in Israeli courts he says what has been taken from him cannot be replaced, what he wants from the case is accountability for those responsible for his family's death. "Money cannot replace what I have lost, I want to know why our home, which was nowhere near any military operations, was targeted, and why my family, who were not involved in politics, were killed."

PCHR submitted a criminal complaint to the Israeli authorities on behalf of the Mousa family on 18 May 2009. To-date, no response has been received

DAY 20
THURS 15᠎ᵀᴴ JANUARY

Today preparing a lecture on Victor Frankl. The students always like the ideas of Frankl. He has been my favourite psychotherapist for many years and his book *Man's Search For Meaning* is a very moving and powerful book which outlines his experiences under the Nazi regime and his therapeutic approach which he called logotherapy. A courageous and compassionate man, he suffered so much in concentration camps during the last world war losing almost his entire family; I imagine he would be very distressed over what is now happening in Gaza.

More about the inauguration of Obama, of course.

THE AL-NADEEM FAMILY

(Official testimony from Palestinian Centre of Human Rights)

"Naser used to help the children with their school work, especially English and mathematics. Now that is my duty. Nothing can compensate me for the loss of my husband. He was always very tender, understanding and calm."

15th January 2009

On 15 January 2009, shortly after 7:00, the Israeli army fired a tank shell and live ammunition at Naser al-Nadeem and his two sons, Bashar (17) and Firas (15), who were fleeing their home in the Tal al-Hawa neighbourhood of Gaza City. The two boys sustained moderate injuries while their father was severely injured. After 9 months of intensive medical treatment in Egypt and Gaza, Naser al-Nadeem eventually succumbed to his wounds. He was 44. Naser's wife, Majda al-Nadeem (45), is now a single parent of three sons, Mohanned (19), Bashar (17), Firas (15), and two daughters, Dima (14) and Tala (9).

A Gaza Diary

"What keeps me going are my children, my children only. I am originally from Damascus and met their father when he was studying there. We married in 1990 and I moved to Gaza with him. I always think to return to Damascus to go and live with my family, but I know that it is better for my children to be here in Gaza. This is their home. I am doing whatever I can to protect them," says Majda as she smiles at her sons.

All the responsibilities of the household are now on Majda's shoulders, both with respect to caring for the children and financially. "Naser used to help the children with their school work, especially English and mathematics. Now that is my duty. Nothing can compensate me for the loss of my husband. He was always very tender, understanding and calm."

Majda explains how she struggles to provide for the most basic needs since Naser died. "My husband used to have an engineering company with a partner and we used to have a good life. Now everything has changed. I am always thinking of how I can provide for my children; how will I bring food, pay for school, electricity, water, everything? I have a lot of pressure on me and it affects me psychologically. We received some payments from the Palestinian Engineers Union and charity organizations but it is not enough or infinite. My family in Syria also tries to help us out financially. They sent us money to repair our house after the war. The bathroom, kitchen, and sewerage were destroyed and there were smoke marks everywhere. Over the past three years our financial situation has gotten worse. A few days ago our electricity was cut off because we cannot pay for the bill."

The children have difficulties in comprehending the changed financial situation. Majda says: "they want to have what the other children have, but I cannot provide it. They also had to leave their [private] school and change to a public school. It has been very difficult for them to adapt to these changes. They are not convinced that I cannot provide them with everything they want."

The physical injuries Bashar and Firas sustained in the attack still mark their daily lives. Firas' right knee was shattered by a bullet. His right leg is shorter as a result and does not bend. Majda explains: "last year doctors placed platinum inside his knee. Now Firas has to wait until he is an adult. Then doctors will check what another surgery can do. But they also said it will never become the way it used to be." Firas says: "I used to play karate with Bashar but I can't do that anymore. I can't really run either. Now I play ping pong."

Bashar had shrapnel wounds in his left leg and right arm, and back. His leg is deformed and sometimes he has pain caused by infections and muscle damage. "Bashar is a very sporting boy. He used to do karate but he changed to gymnastics because of his injuries. Despite his injury, he insists on continuing his sports activities," says his mother.

Because of their injuries Bashar and Firas were not able to go back to school until the following semester. Majda called the Ministry of Education and told them that they had to provide the boys with home schooling; "teachers came to teach mathematics, Arabic and English at home, and the boys managed to end their school year with success."

Despite their optimistic and brave outlook on life, Majda and her children carry with them the psychological scars of the offensive. "The war did change my children. It was a very difficult experience, even for us as adults," she says. "When

A Gaza Diary

we hear explosions we feel fear and remember the war and the attack. If I am afraid, then how must my children be feeling? In the year after his father was killed, Firas would wake up at night and scream 'I want my father'. Now he is older and understands that his father will never come back. The school performances of Bashar and Firas have been affected too. It is getting better, but nothing is as it was before the war. Firas is also held back by his medical treatment."

"We are in need of psychological support," says Majda. "But the people working in this field only visited us for their own interests; taking photos and videos, for the benefit of their organization only." Bashar adds: "once, a psychological worker came to talk with me but I couldn't stay with her. She was the one who needed help. I told her that and then left the room." Majda says: "the only organization I really respect is MSF. The day after the children returned home from the hospital they visited us and kept coming to our house for one year, until the wounds of my children were healed."

When speaking about her outlook on the future, Majda says "I don't have a clear picture of what it will be like. What I am sure about is that I cannot guarantee a nice future for my children. But I am trying to teach my children that education is very important for their future and convince them to do well in school."

Majda is uncertain whether the attack on her family will result in justice in an Israeli court. "They targeted my husband and children, civilians. I am not sure if there will be any result in a court. If there will be any results, they will just make financial compensation and not bring my husband back to life," she says.

A Gaza Diary

PCHR submitted a criminal complaint to the Israeli authorities on behalf of the al-Nadeem family on 23 June 2009. To-date, no response has been received.

DAY 21
FRI 16ᵀᴴ JANUARY

The bombing is continuing and I am too upset to watch any more news about American presidents.

Two Israeli tanks obliterated the house of Dr. Izzeldin Abuelaish in Jabaliya killing his three daughters and a niece. Dr. Abuelaish worked in an Israeli hospital and was a man of peace. Clare and I met him at his talk in Dublin. His wonderful book 'I Shall Not Hate' says it all as to how humankind should behave. He did, however say that he could bear the pain if his personal tragedy would be the end of the killing. As we all know that did not happen.

Decide to read an article by Uri Avnery. On 10 January 2009 he wrote about the lies and propaganda put out by his own Israeli Government justifying the shelling of the UN school in Jabaliya refugee camp. The IDF claimed that Hamas fighters had been firing rockets from near the school entrance. When that was shown to be untrue, the army then claimed that the soldiers had been shot at from within the school compound. Within a few hours it was admitted to UN personnel that this was also a lie. No Hamas fighters were in the school, just terrified refugees. Uri Avnery writes 'Every baby metamorphosed, in the act of dying, into a Hamas terrorist. Every bombed mosque instantly became a Hamas base, every

A Gaza Diary

apartment building an arms cache, every school a terror command post, every civilian building a 'symbol of Hamas rule'. Thus the Israeli army retained its purity as the 'most moral army in the world'.

(In 2023/4 the situation was exactly the same. The Israeli propaganda machine has meant that the mere mention of the word Hamas becomes associated with terrorism so that the international community fails to condemn Israel's killing of thousands of innocent Palestinians. Uri Avnery sadly died a few years ago. I remember interviewing him and his wife, in their home, with my good friend Angela Godfrey-Goldstein. They were such an lovely, impressive couple and his insightful writings are desperately missed in the current ongoing horror).

THE SHURRAB FAMILY

(Official testimony from Palestinian Centre of Human Rights)

"Can i go to a court to restore my sons? No" says Mohammed. "what is the point in bringing the soldiers who killed my sons to justice when there will simply be more and more after them? When others will lose their sons as well? Soldiers commit these crimes because they know they have immunity."

16th January 2009

On 16 January 2009, Israeli forces positioned in the al Fukhari area, south east of Khan Younis, opened fire on the vehicle of Mohammed Shurrab and his two sons Kassab, 28, and Ibrahim, 18, as they were travelling back to their home during the Israeli-declared ceasefire period. Mohammed was injured and crashed the car, his two sons were subsequently shot as they left the car. Israeli soldiers refused to allow medical access to the area, and Kassab and Ibrahim bled to death on the scene over a number of hours. There were no military operations in the area at the time.

A Gaza Diary

For Mohammed Shurrab (67), life since the death of his sons has been a contact battle to fight back the memories of the day. "I try to keep busy in every moment. I read 4-5 hours every day. These books you see on my wall have all been read 2-3 times each. The rest of my time I work on my farm, tend to my crops and care for my live stock", says Mohammed, pointing to the two new born sheep that arrived only two hours beforehand. Despite his best efforts to distract himself, however, Mohammed seems resigned to a life of remembering. "Until I get buried bellow the soil I will continue to suffer, agonising over my sons."

Mohammed is adamant that he hopes that time will come sooner rather than later, "everyday I hope to join my sons. The only question is how I do so. I am a religious man and believe in God, taking my own life would be against my beliefs, but I believe it's better for me to join my sons. I am waiting to die."

His farm, which is on the edge of the Israeli imposed buffer zone along the Gaza – Israeli border, is a hideout from the sights, sounds and issues that bring memories of his sons back to him. "I left my wife and my daughters to come here and live in peace. My wife is very sick. If she is reminded of the incident she will start to scream like she is not human, she cannot breath, she sometimes losses consciousness. I cannot bear to be around her when she is like that."

Despite his best efforts to escape, however, Mohammed is reminded by the smallest detail. "This time of year is the hardest. Everything reminds me of that day. The crisp air, the crops that grow, the dark; everything about this time of year takes me back to the incident." Much like the parents of many others who lost their lives during the Israeli onslaught, Mohammed finds it especially painful to be around those who are around the same age as his sons. "I was at the wedding of my young cousin recently. He is the same age as Ibrahim would have been if he was still alive. I couldn't stop thinking of all the things that he could have done with his life if it wasn't taken from him; education, marriage, children, now he can do none of this."

Muhammad has suffered both mentally and physically as a result of stress and physical injuries incurred due to the shooting. Shuffling slowly and carefully around his farm house home, his physical symptoms are obvious. "I had severe damage to my neural system as a result of the attack," says Mohammed, "my balance is now destroyed." Lifting his top to show the long scar running down his back where he had surgery to repair his injuries Muhammad says his ability to fight infection and illness has deteriorated since the attack. The stress he feels as a result of his experience has left him unable to sleep and he is forced to take sleeping pills to steal a brief 4 to 5 hours of sleep every night before waking very early in the morning.

Soon, Mohammed's remaining sons and daughters will be fully educated and independent. Mohammed says when that time comes his work is done and there is nothing left keeping him from the afterlife. "The moment my children say we need for nothing, that's it, I have done everything I am responsible for, I can go," says Mohammed. "The good times have gone, they will not be back. I hope for nothing". When asked what his greatest fear for the future is, Mohammed replies; "my fear is a future."

Regarding the pursuit of justice within Israeli courts Mohammed is scornful. "Absolutely not; the soldier who killed my sons did not act in a vacuum. He had permission from his superiors. What is more their crimes are ongoing. Stories like mine are not isolated incidences." Any redress in Israeli courts, for Mohammed, were it forthcoming, would be irrelevant in any case. "Can I go to a court to restore my sons? No" says Mohammed. "What is the point in bringing the soldiers who killed my sons to justice when there will simply be more and more after them? When others will lose their sons as well? Soldiers commit these crimes because they know they have immunity."

PCHR submitted a criminal complaint to the Israeli authorities on behalf of the Shurrab family on 19 August 2009. To-date, no response has been received.

DAY 22
SAT 17ᵀᴴ JANUARY

Operation Cast Lead is over! What a relief, although Gaza is devastated. Around 1440 Palestinians are dead, 3 Israeli civilians and ten Israeli soldiers, most of whom were killed by friendly fire. Who is the victim here? Just do the maths! Rebuilding Gaza will take a very long time. As occupiers, Israel is responsible for any damage in the Strip but they always refuse to pay and the rebuilding is left to foreign governments. Why the bombing has finally come to an end today, I just do not know.

(In 2024 when discussing the South African submission to the ICJ, Professor Francis Boyle of Illinois university alleged that the people working with Obama requested an end to Operation Cast Lead in order not to spoil the inauguration on January 20. If so, that is a total disgrace as it means that the Americans could have ended the carnage at any time and could have saved so many innocent lives. That also means that the 2023/4 massacre could be ended immediately if Biden were to refuse to supply weapons and demand a permanent ceasefire.)

THE AL ASHQAR FAMILY

(Official testimony from Palestinian Centre of Human Rights)

"Madleen refuses to sleep by herself; she will only sleep in her parent's room" says nujoud, "she's afraid to be by herself at all. The other day we were in the garden and i asked her to go to the bedroom to bring something. She refused to go without me."

17th January 2009

On 17 January 2009, at approximately 05:30, the area surrounding the UNRWA school in Beit Lahiya came under attack from Israeli forces. The area was bombarded using both high explosive, and white phosphorous artillery; white phosphorous is an incendiary chemical which ignites on contact with oxygen, its use in civilian populated areas violates the principle of distinction, and the prohibition of indiscriminate attacks. Nujoud Al Ashqar, along with approximately 1,600 others, was taking shelter in the school at

A Gaza Diary

the time of the attack. Nujoud sustained severe head injuries as a result of the bombing, and also losing her right hand. Two of her sons Bilal, 6, and Muhammed, 4, were killed in the attack.

When PCHR first spoke to Nujoud in the aftermath of the attack three years ago, her life had become extremely difficult, particularly her relationship with her husband, Mohammed. "At first my husband blamed me for the death of the boys. He used to threaten me every day that he would re-marry" says Nujoud, "but things have got better between us since the birth of our daughter Haneen. He loves her deeply and she loves him."

Nujoud's daughter Haneen, 1, was both a blessing and a severe challenge for Nujoud, who, despite being thankful she was able to give birth to another child after the loss of Muhammed and Bilal, is faced with extreme difficulties caring for herself, the household and her children given the loss of her arm and other medical difficulties following the attack. "I get most frustrated when trying to care for Haneen" says Nujoud, "I need help form my daughter Madleen all the time to care for her. I always feel sad for her because she sacrifices so much of her education to care for the house and her sister. But I need her to do it" says Nujoud. "Her grades in school have suffered as a result. It's made worse by the fact I find myself with no patience to help her with her school work anymore since the attack."

Madleen was herself in the UNRWA school at the time of the attack and faces difficulties with both the memory of that day and the loss of Bilal and Muhammed. "Madleen refuses to sleep by herself; she will only sleep in her parent's room," says Nujoud, "she's afraid to be by herself at all. The other day we were in the garden and I asked her to go to the bedroom to bring something. She refused to go without me."

A Gaza Diary

Nujoud shares Madleen's fear of the past and apprehension of the future. "Sometimes when there are rumours of a new war or Israeli incursions Madleen will start asking me about it and speaking of the incident. But I can't bear to talk with her about what happened and I just ask her not to talk about it.". The memory of the attack remains so moving for Nujoud that she does not speak with it to anybody. "Sometimes visitors will come over and ask to hear about that night. I don't talk to them about it though. If I do I will spend the rest of the day and the whole night going over it in my head."

Apart from the loss of one hand Nujoud has been left with severe pain in her head. When PCHR spoke to her three years ago she would wear her head scarf everywhere, including inside the house, as she had lost all her hair due to severe burns. "Now most of my hair has grown back" says Nujoud, "except for small patches due to injuries, but still when Madleen combs my hair I'm in agony."

The loss of Bilal and Muhammed is especially painful for Nujoud. "I could never forget my children. If I stayed alive for 200,000 years I would not forget them." Bilal and Muhammed were always a huge pillar of stability and support in Nujoud's life. "When I used to get angry with my husband I would want to leave the house and go to my family. Bilal and Muhammed would calm me down and get me to stay. Now, when my husband and I argue, I just go to my room and think of them." For Nujoud's husband, Muhammed, who is deaf and dumb, the loss of Bilal, who used to help him communicate with others outside the house, was also devastating.

With another child on the way, Nujoud is hopeful for her health and for another baby boy in the future, who she also plans to call Bilal. "Me and my husband had been waiting for

A Gaza Diary

Bilal, he was so dear to our hearts, I hope to have a son so I can name him after his brother."

PCHR submitted a criminal complaint to the Israeli authorities on behalf of the Al Ashqar family on 18 May 2012. PCHR have received an interlocutory response noting receipt of the original complaint. To date, however, and despite repeated requests, no further information has been communicated to PCHR, regarding the status of any investigation, and so on.

Epilogue

In spring 2009 there appeared to be a glimmer of hope following the terrible devastation in Gaza. The UN Human Rights Council established a Fact Finding Mission to investigate possible violations of international law. The four person mission was headed by the South African judge, Richard Goldstone, who had been a chief prosecutor in the tribunals investigating war crimes in Rwanda and the former Yugoslavia.

The members of the inquiry team visited Gaza in late May and early June 2009. Israel refused to cooperate with the inquiry and would not let them enter Gaza from Israel. The Goldstone Report was the result of the inquiry and detailed alleged war crimes committed by the Israeli military as well as by Palestinian armed groups who had launched rocket attacks against Israeli civilians.

Among the specific allegations of violations of international law were:

The massacre of the Samouni family, when Israeli soldiers ordered around 100 members of the Samouni family into a single building.in Gaza City. Soldiers held the family for 24 hours before shelling the building on 4 January 2009. More than twenty members of the family were killed.

'White Flag' killings where documented by the UN mission and human rights groups. Several witnesses saw Israeli soldiers kill Palestinians who were fleeing while carrying makeshift white flags. (In 2024 a British news channel showed

A Gaza Diary

soldiers killing one man and injuring another while blood seeped into the white flag. The IDF still know they can act with impunity.)

Use of white phosphorus: there were numerous cases of the use of the incendiary substance white phosphorus in populated areas. It is illegal to use this substance in crowded locations. (There have also been accusations of the use of white phosphorous in the 2023/4 assault.)

Richard Goldstone was viciously attacked for his report, by Israel and by his own Jewish community in South Africa. Because of his Jewish/Zionist credentials it was thought that Israel would be unable to make the usual accusations of anti-semitism against him. When these accusations failed there was an attempt to destroy his reputation which was impeccable and difficult to destroy. All these disgraceful pressures, however, were obviously having a terrible effect on Goldstone himself and his family - two years later he effectively disowned his own report.

Norman Finkelstein in his amazingly detailed academic book *Gaza - An Inquest Into Its Martyrdom* says that talking of Operation Cast Lead as a protracted land war was not at all correct: "Hamas was barely equipped, barely present in the conflict zones, and barely engaged by Israeli forces except when it could not fight back". In the same way, the Israeli Air Force could boast that it suffered no damage from its bombing raids. That is because Gaza had no air defence of any sort. Indeed, Gaza's single small airport had been put out of action and destroyed by Israeli bombing six years previously. The Israeli Air Force, meanwhile, is one of the most sophisticated and well-equipped in the world and in 2023/4 both the UK and US showed no hesitation in reinforcing its supplies of every kind of advanced weaponry - including blockbuster bombs which were never intended for use in civilian residential areas.

As a result of Goldstone's retraction, Prime Minister Benjamin Netanyahu, was able to say both then and in 2023/4 that the IDF is the most moral army in the world that never contravenes the rules of war. The result of Goldstone's action was as Finkelstein writes: "a black day for human rights and a red-letter day for their transgressors. Might had yet again brought right to its knees". As for Goldstone he says: "The inescapable fact was that he killed the Report, and simultaneously lowered the curtain on his own career". Politicians beware!

I do not think that Israel has succeeded in any of its aims in Gaza in 2023/4. Its so-called main objective of destroying Hamas was never going to happen because Hamas is an ideology, not just a group of armed militants; the destruction of Gaza and the massacre of its inhabitants is only going to make this ideology more powerful everywhere. Other militant groups are now basing their violence on the occupation of Palestine and making the world a more unstable place.

The second stated aim of Israel is the return of its hostages which is, of course, entirely legitimate and much to be desired. There can be no denying that Hamas broke international law by taking innocent Israeli civilians as hostages. Everything seemed to be going quite well initially when a hostage and prisoner release deal was negotiated. Now, however, intensified military force seems to be Israel's preferred method of negotiation - despite thereby greatly increasing the risks for the existing hostages and being devastating for Gaza's population. Indeed, at least three Israeli hostages are known to have been shot by their own soldiers when trying to escape. It is also understood that an operation to release two hostages in

A Gaza Diary

the Rafah area resulted in the deaths of approximately one hundred innocent Palestinians resident in the locality. At the time of writing there have been no more prisoner exchanges and more and more Palestinians continue to be imprisoned and tortured in the West Bank. It is strange that the IDF do not seen to be worried that their inhumane strategy of carpet-bombing Gaza will in all likelihood lead to the further deaths of Israeli hostages.

Neither of Netanyahu's aims have been achieved but many thousands of Palestinians are dead and many thousands of children have lost limbs and their entire families. Despite these atrocities, Israel continues to claim victimhood as it has done since the foundation of the State of Israel. The real victims are of course the occupied, not the occupiers.

It is becoming increasingly obvious that ethnic cleansing may well be one of the motivations for Israel's actions in Gaza. Over recent months, several members of the Israeli Government have said as much, although officially this has always been denied. It has nevertheless been reliably reported that approaches have been made to certain South American countries offering them a mere 300 dollars per person if they would accept any potential refugees from Gaza.

Maybe the latest massacre will finally convince the world leaders to do the correct thing and call for a permanent ceasefire. Maybe they will also call for an end to the illegal occupation and allow an investigation to take place that will be free to tell the truth - and not intimidated as happened to Goldstone after 2009. Just maybe, the very real threat of a global war and the devastating destruction of our planet will play a part in the search for a just solution. Sadly, it would seem that most politicians around the world are more interested in their political survival than ethical considerations.

A Gaza Diary

In 2006, Jeff Halper, Israeli Coordinator of the Israeli Committee Against House Demolitions, wrote in the preface of *The Resting Place Of The Moon* that we must "advocate for the good in terms of pressuring our governments to end the Occupation now, before one more person dies, before one more house is demolished, before the Holy Land becomes so barren from the bulldozers and tanks of the military that, alas, there are no more branches upon which birds can perch and hold their consultations". Maybe people's protests for peace and justice across the world - especially the courageous voices of progressive Jewish communities - will help politicians to finally realise that their own interests and those of the world generally may best be served by behaving with honesty and integrity: and always doing the right thing.

As the late much-respected Uri Avnery said in 2009: "What will be seared into the consciousness of the world will be the image of Israel as a blood-stained monster, ready at any moment to commit war crimes and not prepared to abide by any moral restraints. This will have severe consequences for our long-term future, our standing in the world, our chance of achieving peace and quiet."

Perhaps those who still believe that Israel has a right to act in its own 'self-defence' by committing war crimes should listen to Israeli journalist Gideon Levy who in a recent headline in the Israeli newspaper Ha'aretz says: '*If It Isn't a Genocide in Gaza, Then What Is It?*'

It is difficult to disagree with this eminent Israeli journalist. The failure to act by world leaders has brought shame on us all.

F.H. MARCH 2024

Mistruths in Gaza

(Published in the Irish Times, 8th Nov 2023)

The UN secretary-general, Antonio Guterres, told the UN security council on 24 October that in his opinion the horrific attack by Hamas on Israeli civilians on 7 October "did not happen in a vacuum". Israel has rejected this claim in the strongest terms by calling for his resignation and has threatened to reject all visa applications by UN officials. Regrettably, some western leaders have joined in this criticism of Guterres. The purpose of this article is to establish the facts on which the secretary-general's remarks were based.

It is well established that truth is the greatest casualty of war; this is certainly the context in which the appalling tragedy is currently unfolding before us in Gaza. The universal use of social media and the widespread access to fake videos and falsified information have created a minefield for reputable journalists and news agencies attempting to determine precisely what is happening.

It is also important, however, to establish the precise facts of how Israel's occupation of Gaza took place and how Hamas seized control of the territory from the Palestinian authority.

Historical background

For centuries, Gaza has been little more than a stopping point on journeys from the cities of the Nile to the Levant. It was the route that the British general Edmund Allenby took to capture the holy land from the Ottomans in 1917/18. It was only with the partition of British-ruled Palestine in 1948 that Gaza sprang

A Gaza Diary

into political significance. Israel's victory in its war of independence resulted in the mass migration to Gaza of refugees from nearby Arab majority towns such as Beersheba, Ashkelon and Jaffa (all of which had been allocated to a new Arab state under the partition plan). This new area then fell under the administration of Egypt and became known as the Gaza strip. It currently has a population of over 2.2 million in an area of 388 square kilometres (by comparison this is less than half the size of Louth - Ireland's smallest county). Egypt, in its wisdom, never claimed sovereignty over any part of Gaza and has clearly stated it has no desire to do so now.

Israel's overwhelming victory in the six day Yom Kippur war of 1967 led to its occupation of Gaza (as well as the west bank and the Golan heights). Despite strident claims to the contrary, Israel has never really left any of these territories.

The building of Jewish settlements soon followed - expropriating some of the best agricultural land and exploiting the strip's meagre water resources. I visited Gaza as part of my official duties when these settlements were in full production and to call them a blot on the landscape - in the midst of the overcrowded and impoverished local population - would have been a gross understatement.

Under enormous pressure from both Washington and Brussels, Israel eventually agreed to withdraw the Gaza settlements in 2005 as part of the implementation of the peace process established by the Oslo accords. However, the manner in which this withdrawal took place proved to be of very little benefit to the local people - or indeed to the Palestinian

A Gaza Diary

authority which was officially responsible for taking over the settlements. Much of the buildings and agricultural infrastructure had been destroyed before the settlers left. More importantly, Israel began to impose increasingly restrictive conditions and delays on the export of fresh produce from Gaza to Israel and to international markets. This resulted in the wastage of large quantities of tomatoes, strawberries and fresh flowers (apparently Gaza is one of the most suitable places on earth for the growing of carnation flowers!). Israel claimed to have withdrawn from the Gaza strip but in practical terms nothing could have been further from the truth: the Israelis continued to maintain complete control over the land, sea and air borders of the strip.

The consequent damage done to the standing and reputation of the Palestinian authority no doubt contributed to the Hamas victory in the parliamentary elections held at Washington's insistence in January 2006. Without the necessary support from Israel or the west, the legitimate Palestinian administration was hounded out of Gaza by a bloody Hamas coup the following year.

Although the Israeli government may claim otherwise, it is widely acknowledged that right-wing elements in Israel (including Benjamin Netanyahu) welcomed the Hamas coup and rejoiced in the fact that there was no longer a united Palestinian leadership with which to negotiate. It also gave Israel a carte blanche to treat the population of Gaza with even greater disregard and brutality than before. The result has been an increasing deterioration of the Gazan economy accompanied by a steady stream of violence and casualties

A Gaza Diary

(mainly on the Palestinian side) for the past fifteen years or more.

UN Secretary-General

The statement made by secretary-general Guterres was accordingly based on considerable and substantive evidence. Its rejection by the Israeli government (and others) can only be described as self-deception. So long as this self-deception continues, it is difficult to see how the current conflagration can be resolved. It will certainly not be resolved by committing further war crimes, whether by massive bombardment of civilian areas by Israel or indiscriminate launching of rockets and hostage-taking by Hamas. The longer it takes for a ceasefire to be put in place - as demanded by 120 UN member states and the secretary-general - the harder it will be to achieve the political compromise which will eventually have to be found. The only alternative is further death and destruction which can benefit no-one.

Unless the words of Antonio Guterres are taken to heart by all the main players, the prospects of any just or lasting solution in Gaza or the region generally must remain very slim.

The author, Dr Niall Holohan, is a retired Irish diplomat. He was based in Ramallah as the Government's Representative to the Palestinian authority from 2002 to 2006. He has also served at the UN and as the Irish Ambassador to Saudi Arabia, Oman, Yemen, Iraq and Bahrain.

Printed in Great Britain
by Amazon